The ENVIRONMENT

Patricia Lovett

Batsford Academic and Educational Ltd London

Contents

Typset by Tek-Art Ltd, London SE 20
and printed in Great Britain by
R. J. Acford
Chichester, Sussex
for the publishers
Batsford Academic and Educational Ltd,
an imprint of B T Batsford Ltd,
4 Fitzhardinge Street
London W1H 0AH

ISBN 0 7134 3580 1

Acknowledgment

The Author and Publishers would like to thank
the following for their kind permission to
reproduce copyright illustrations in this book:
Aerofilms Ltd, pages 30, 36, 48 (bottom);
J. Allan Cash Ltd, pages 11 (top), 17, 34
(left), 55, 65; Barnaby's Picture Library,
pages 4, 9, 18, 20, 21, 43 (bottom); Bilsom
International Ltd, page 16; British Waterways
Board, page 51; Camera Press Ltd, page 11
(bottom); GLC, pages 43 (top), 49 (top);
Richard and Sally Greenhill, pages 42, 63;
Mustapha Karkouti, page 59; Keystone Press
Agency Ltd, pages 7, 12, 19, 29 (top), 45, 48
(top), 49 (bottom), 52, 64; North West Water,
page 23; Peak Park Joint Planning Board, page
38; Popperfoto, page 54; RSPB, page 29
(bottom) (photograph by Michael W.
Richards); Thames Water Authority, page 24;
John Topham Picture Library, pages 6 (left),
27, 32, 34 (right), 37, 57 (bottom), 60. The
photographs on page 46 are copyright of the
Author. The maps and diagrams on pages 6,
14, 41 and 61 were drawn by Rudolph Britto;
those on pages 10, 13, 37 and 40 by Patricia
Lovett. Thanks are due to Peta Hambling and
to Patricia Mandel for the picture research on
the book.

Introduction

All living things — plants, animals, insects — are surrounded by their ENVIRONMENT*. The environment *is* the surroundings. The environment for sea creatures and fish is water; the environment for flying insects is the air; the environment for plants includes not only the soil and air, but the climate and weather, too. The environment affects growth and development.

The plants and animals which share the same environment are part of an ECOSYSTEM. When the environment changes, so too may the plants and animals and also, of course, the ecosystem. Most ecosystems are very complex. The ecosytem of a forest includes many different birds, insects, plants and animals, as well as the trees. Within that ecosystem are many FOOD CHAINS. A food chain is a way of transferring energy. For example, in a forest the trees use the sun's energy to grow; insects feed on the leaves of the trees, will be eaten by birds, and the birds will be eaten by a fox. In each stage the energy from the sun has been transferred and used. *Nature is able to keep a balance* in the ecosystem because of the food chains. If there were no food chains, then there would be an imbalance. In our example, if the birds did not eat insects, then there would be so many insects eating the leaves of the trees that the trees would eventually die.

Nature is able to deal with WASTE as well. Every autumn, millions of leaves fall off trees, they decay, and are gradually turned into soil. Plants use the carbon dioxide breathed out by animals and give out oxygen, by PHOTO-SYNTHESIS. It is when people interfere with the environment that the natural balance is threatened.

*Words in CAPITALS are explained in the Glossary, pages 66-68.

We rely on our environment for three essential NATURAL RESOURCES: first, living things — plants and animals; second, materials such as metals, coal, oil and gas; third, energy — this is the power to do work, and comes in many forms, such as electricity, heat and NUCLEAR POWER. We also like to keep our environment attractive. People change the environment by using more of one thing than another, and so making an imbalance. Producing more waste than nature can cope with affects the balance. Changing the environment for the worse is POLLUTION. Pollution can slow down the growth rate of plants and animals; it can interfere with people's amenities or comfort, and it can affect their health. Some pollution is TOXIC — this means it is poisonous and can kill. Preventing, or cutting down pollution costs money. In recent years, people have realized how harmful pollution is, and individuals and industries have taken steps to prevent it, as we shall see in this book.

People have also become more aware of how the environment has been affected by change. Some changes have made an improvement. Derelict building sites in cities have been made into gardens and playgrounds for children, for example. CONSERVATION is protecting areas of land, buildings, animals, plants and so on from harm and change. In these cases, a decision is made about *what* should be conserved, and *how* to go about this. Not everyone always agrees about what is worth preserving. People make value judgements about conservation. There are no hard-and-fast guidelines.

This book looks at various parts of the environment in Britain, what the problems are, how they have been tackled so far, and what can be done in the future.

Air

There has always been air POLLUTION. Even before there was any life on the earth, volcanoes erupted, throwing lava and ash into the air. This ash and poisonous sulphur gases would have suffocated any living creature. Strong winds blowing dust across the land, tornadoes, whirlwinds, and dust-devils also pollute the air. So does plant pollen. Anyone who suffers from hay fever will know this from experience.

CLEAN AIR is essential for us to live. Although all air naturally contains some impurities — dust, spores, water vapour — these usually do no harm.

Air is a mixture of gases: 78% nitrogen; 21% oxygen; 0.03% carbon dioxide; and small amounts of other gases — argon, neon, helium, etc.

Oxygen in this mixture is the most important gas to us. We breathe in air and, in our lungs, about 4% of the oxygen from it is exchanged for carbon dioxide, which we breathe out. This process is called RESPIRATION. If this was all that happened, the amount of oxygen in the air would decrease over the years; and the amount of carbon dioxide would increase. But, in fact, another natural process keeps the balance. In sunlight green plants take in carbon dioxide, in exchange for oxygen. This process is called PHOTOSYNTHESIS. Obviously it is important to have enough areas with green plants to produce oxygen. It is also important to have sunlight. But some air pollution kills green plants; and other air pollution causes SMOG or a haze which blocks out the sunlight.

A tornado in Minneapolis, USA. The people living in these houses will be affected by the tornado in many ways. The dust in the air makes it difficult to see, and makes people choke. It is blown into their houses and sometimes gets into machinery and cars as well.

People have been concerned about air pollution in England for a long time:

In 1273 Laws were made to stop the burning of coal in London. It was "prejudicial" to health.

1578 Queen Elizabeth I "findeth hersealfe greatly greved and annoyed with the taste and smoke of the sea-cooles".

1648 Londoners asked Parliament to stop coal being brought from Newcastle because of their health.

1661 John Evelyn wrote "Fumifugium" — or "The smoke of London Dissipated". He suggested that London should be a SMOKELESS ZONE, with a "GREENBELT" around the centre.

1853-56 Smoke Abatement Acts for Metropolitan areas.

1875
1891 } Public Health Acts, for Smoke Abate-
1926 } ment.
1936

1951 Coventry first smokeless zone in Britain, where only smokeless fuel, such as gas, oil, and smokeless coal and coke can be burnt in domestic fires; and where there were also similar restrictions for industrial fuel, and the smoke and dust they were allowed to make.

1952 4,000 DIED IN LONDON SMOGS.

1955 City of London said to be a smokeless zone.

1956 Clean Air Act I.

1968 Clean Air Act II — addition to first Act.

1970 Some smoke control orders suspended due to smokeless coal shortage — European Conservation Year.

The Clean Air Acts of 1956 and 1968 said that:

(i) No dark smoke should be given off from industrial chimneys.

(ii) Air and dust from furnaces and certain industries should be reduced as much as possible.

(iii) There should be smoke-controlled zones.

THE CAUSES OF AIR POLLUTION

When something is burnt, it uses oxygen from the air. Often the oxygen combines with other chemicals, and gases such as carbon monoxide and carbon dioxide are formed. These gases go into the air with other waste products, which we may see as smoke. Smoke pollutes the air, and the waste gases, especially carbon monoxide are TOXIC and dangerous to breathe.

Most of the smoke which worried people from the earliest times came from burning coal. When ordinary bituminous coal is burnt in grates at home, the smoke contains tiny droplets of tar. Breathed in, this tar, and small pieces of black carbon compounds, can cause cancer of the lungs.

In certain conditions on cold, clear nights in winter, a FOG is formed. When there is a lot of air pollution from smoke, the smoke and fog together make SMOG. In London this yellow smog was called a "pea-souper" (after thick, yellow, pea soup). There were a lot of pea-soupers in the nineteenth and the first half of the twentieth century.

In 1952 there was a very bad smog in London which lasted for five days. People could hardly see at all during this smog. Policemen had to direct traffic at traffic-lights, because drivers could not see the lights change. In the cinema people could not see the screen, and a couple of people even fell off the ends of jetties into the River Thames. Worst of all were the 4,000 deaths due to bronchitis and other chest infections which occurred during the smog. These deaths were a result of the bad smog. (See the graph on page 6.)

Bonfires too cause air pollution. The leaves, branches and rubbish burnt in bonfires at home and on building sites often do not completely burn. This is most obvious when a

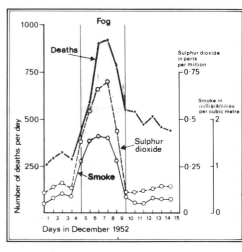

This photograph of Ludgate Circus in London was taken at 2.00 pm on 6 December 1952. Although the street lights are switched on, and the bus has its headlights on full beam, it is still difficult to see the man standing on a traffic island. Traffic lights, the kerb and the pavement are invisible.

This graph shows the period of time from 1-15 December 1952. There was fog from 5-9 December — shown by the shaded area. The other lines show that smoke and sulphur dioxide (SO_2) increased significantly at this time. The thick line shows the number of deaths — which also increased greatly during this period.

piece of paper is carried up with the smoke. The edges of the paper are red, and the rest is black. The paper breaks into hundreds of tiny fragments which all pollute the air. There are always a lot of smuts in the air the day after Guy Fawkes night. In some areas bonfires are banned completely, because of smokeless zones. In other areas bonfires are only allowed after dusk — although it is difficult to understand the reason for this. Bonfires pollute no matter when they are lit.

Many people today are becoming more and more worried about the amount of air pollution caused by cars and lorries. Buses and lorries run on diesel oil, or derv. This is heavy fuel, which is not as volatile as petrol. Sometimes the pollution from these vehicles can be seen easily — as they struggle up a steep hill in low gear. It is most unpleasant sitting in a car behind a lorry giving off a lot of exhaust. The exhaust from cars is not so obvious, but can be seen usually on cold mornings or when the car is not properly tuned.

Burning petrol or derv in an engine produces a number of substances:

Carbon dioxide
Carbon monoxide
Lead
Nitrogen oxides
Sulphur oxides
Hydrocarbons
Smoke particles

Carbon dioxide is used by plants in PHOTO-SYNTHESIS. This is explained on page 4. As more vehicles are used, more carbon dioxide is produced. There may come a time when the green plants cannot cope with all the carbon dioxide being produced in some areas. Some scientists are especially worried about this gas. The amount of it in the air has increased by 15% in the last hundred years. A layer of carbon dioxide may eventually form above the earth, acting like the glass of a greenhouse, trapping in heat. This is called the GREEN-HOUSE EFFECT. As the earth became warmer, the ice caps would melt and the sea level would rise by as much as 60-70 metres. This would flood London and most of the world's big cities.

Carbon monoxide is a poisonous gas. Breathed in, it kills by taking the place of oxygen in the blood, and stopping oxygen from getting to the body tissue. At 1,000 parts per million (p.p.m.) of air, it will kill very quickly. In industry the legal limit is 30 p.p.m. Measurements taken in the Rotherhithe Tunnel in London registered 500 p.p.m. and there were 280 p.p.m. in Oxford Street. Policemen on traffic duty in Tokyo, Japan, always wear masks. They can only do traffic duty for half an hour, because of the pollution, and then breathe oxygen from cylinders at the side of the road. Many drivers in Japan also wear masks.

Tetraethyl lead is added to petrol to make cars run more smoothly and efficiently — it is an anti-knock agent. Lead is a dangerous poison. It is accumulative. This means that when it is absorbed from the air into the body it stays there, and does not pass through like other substances. It gradually builds up until it can do a lot of harm, and can cause death. The amount of lead in the air has increased rapidly over the years. Scientists found that the ice formed in Greenland in 1940 had four times the lead content of ice formed in 1750. And from 1940 to 1968 the amount of lead in the ice in Greenland increased by 300%. Most of this lead is thought to be from car exhaust from industrial countries in the northern hemisphere. Other tests carried out near Birmingham also produced worrying results. Doctors tested the lead level in the blood of children living near the Gravelly Hill (Spaghetti Junction) Interchange. In two years, from 1972-74, the lead content had increased from 12.2 micrograms per 100 millilitres to 26.3 micrograms. It is thought that at 30 to 40 micrograms there is serious damage to children's health, including brain damage.

A peculiar smog is formed by hydrocarbons and nitrogen oxide in the air. It is not like the pea-soupers that used to occur in London, because it is found in hot places, such as Los Angeles, USA. It looks like a brownish haze, and irritates the eyes, nose and throat. In strong sunlight the oxygen in the air reacts

Police Pollution Squads check car exhaust in Japan. Any car which gives out more than 5.5% of carbon monoxide in its exhaust has an "out of order" sticker put on it. The owner must have the car repaired without delay and report again to the police. If the order is ignored, then the owner is fined and loses his licence.

with the hydrocarbons and nitrogen oxide to form this smog, which is called a PHOTO-CHEMICAL SMOG because it only occurs in sunlight.

Sulphur dioxide is often used as an indicator of the air pollution in an area. It is not only harmful to plants, animals and humans, but can also be converted into sulphuric acid in a damp atmosphere. The sulphuric acid, breathed in, penetrates deep into our lungs. It also wears away buildings and metal.

As well as car and lorry exhausts, industry has often been blamed for causing air pollution. The Clean Air Acts have reduced some of the air pollution — look back at page 5. Tall chimneys prevent pollution from falling on the land around a factory, but the air is polluted eventually. Norway and Sweden are being affected by acid in the air which they say comes from Britain. This makes the trees grow more slowly. Rain is becoming more acid, and so are the lakes in these two countries.

People who live near and work in some industries feel that the Clean Air Acts have done very little. Houses, plants and trees close to a cement works are often covered in a fine white dust. The health of coalminers and workers in asbestos factories is sometimes affected by the polluted air.

Tobacco pollutes the air too. It causes disease and sometimes death to those people who smoke cigarettes, cigars or a pipe. Non-smokers who sit in a smoke-filled atmosphere have to suffer air pollution caused by the selfish behaviour of others.

The chemical chlorine which is used in aerosol sprays, affects ozone. The chlorine is thought to be a potential hazard to the OZONE SHIELD around the earth. If the ozone shield is reduced, then skin cancer caused by RADIATION may increase. These chemicals have been banned in some states in the USA.

Some aeroplanes affect the atmosphere, too. It is thought that Concorde, in particular, has changed the ozone shield.

THE EFFECTS OF AIR POLLUTION

Air pollution causes disease and death to people. The smog in 1952 was responsible for the deaths of 4,000. The dirt which pollutes the air gets into our lungs. Someone who lives in the country, away from industry and traffic, has pink lungs; a town-dweller has grey lungs. Breathing in grit, smuts and sulphuric acid causes irritation in the lungs. Often to cough removes the irritation, but it can also worsen the condition of those with weak chests and bronchitis.

Some pollutants are more harmful than others. FIBROSIS is a disease where the lung tissues are scarred by breathing in dust. Coal dust causes PNEUMOCONIOSIS, and stone dust SILICOSIS. All these conditions make breathing very difficult. Some men with miner's lung (pneumoconiosis) cannot walk upstairs. They are always short of breath, and find any movement painful. People who work with asbestos sometimes develop ASBESTOSIS where the lungs are scarred and cancerous. Even a short exposure to blue asbestos can lead to asbestosis — which may develop many years later. Blue asbestos is so dangerous that it is now banned in Britain.

In towns and cities houses have to be painted and decorated more often than in the country. The dirty air makes paintwork look grubby. Acid pollution eats into curtains and furnishings, so that they do not last so long. Clothes, too, get dirtier and have to be washed more often in towns.

Air pollution affects animals in the same ways as people. It can stunt their growth, get into their lungs and may eventually kill them. The effect of pollution on animals is particularly worrying because some animals are part of our FOOD CHAIN. Animals absorb pollutants by breathing them in as well as by eating grass or food stuffs which may be contaminated. We eat the animals and animal products and so, in turn, take the pollution into our bodies.

Brick and phosphate works and aluminium

smelters give off fluorides into the air. When enough fluorides fall on grass, which is then eaten by animals, there can be horrifying results. The first sign of FLUOROSIS is that the animals lose their teeth; this is followed by swollen joints, where the bones have grown, and, eventually, lameness and considerable pain.

People have known for some time that air pollution affects plants. It can harm plants in three ways. First of all, the dirt in the air is deposited on the leaves, blocking the holes through which the plant "breathes". Secondly, sulphur dioxide in the air combines with water to make an acid. Even in very low concentrations this can still burn and DEFOLIATE (remove the leaves of) a plant. Lastly, by causing smogs or hazes, air pollution prevents the sun getting to plants, which is essential for PHOTOSYNTHESIS.

Many old buildings are made of limestone. Acids produced as a result of air pollution attack limestone, which is mainly calcium carbonate. Buildings are covered in dirt, carvings and sculptures are eaten away, and any metals are corroded unless they are covered by paint or plastic. A lot of buildings are being cleaned and restored. The dirt is "sand-blasted" away — a mixture of sand, water and detergent is used. Sometimes the badly eroded carvings are replaced by fibre-glass or special plastic ones.

PREVENTING AIR POLLUTION

Air pollution has been much reduced since the Clean Air Acts. Towns and cities are cleaner and pleasanter places to live and work in. The main effects of the Clean Air Acts were the introduction of SMOKELESS ZONES and the controlling of smoke from industry. Gas, oil, electricity and smokeless solid fuel have replaced coal. It seems as though there is still some room for improvement for industry. It is possible to treat the waste gases from factories before discharging them into the air. They can either be "scrubbed" by fine jets of water, which remove most of the dirt; or an electric current can be passed through. This removes most of the dust particles.

Petrol- and derv-powered vehicles pollute the atmosphere. There have been experiments with battery cars, cars driven on methane gas, hydrogen and alcohol, and buses powered by electricity. At present, apart from milk floats, the electric car does not seem feasible. British cars for export to America have to have special anti-pollution devices fitted. We could ask why these are not standard in Britain.

On a more personal level, we could all help to prevent air pollution. Walking and cycling are two ways of getting around which do not pollute at all. Using public transport, when available, also helps to reduce pollution, and CONSERVE energy. Try to avoid using aerosols. Under Common Law it is possible to take action against a factory which affects your home through smoke, fumes or bad smells. Compost rubbish to avoid burning it on bonfires.

This building is being cleaned by sand-blasting. The man on the ladder holds a hose which carries a mixture of sand, water and detergent. The stone on the building can be scrubbed clean. It is easy to see the effects of air pollution in this photograph — compare the cleaned area with the dirty part.

A Breathing Space

For a long time the Amazon Basin in Brazil was one of the largest unspoilt natural areas in the world. Much of it is dense jungle which is very difficult to get through. The rivers twist and turn, and there are poisonous insects and snakes. People use small aeroplanes and helicopters to get from one place to another.

Tribes of Indians live in the jungle. They catch fish, hunt wild animals and may do a little farming. Their houses are made out of wood from the trees, grass and mud. Their way of life is well suited to the wildness of the environment.

The government in Brazil decided that they

This map shows the huge area of the Amazon. The route of the Trans-Amazonica road has been marked. ▼

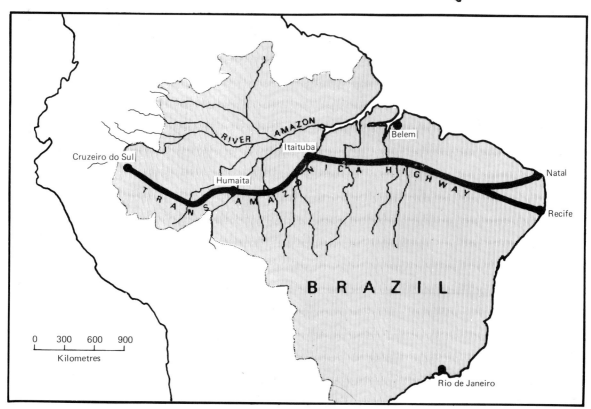

These Ticuna Indian children live by the river and get all they need from the surroundings. Their way of life is balanced with their environment.

The jungle must be cleared to build roads, so opening up the area for development. Notice how much land is used in building a two-lane road. The cleared area on the right will soon be useless, as the soil is quickly washed away by the heavy rain.

▼

would like a road to go across the country — the Trans-Amazonica Highway. To do this, first of all they had to move the Indians to other areas and sometimes into reservations. Many of the Indians found the move difficult to cope with. Some caught diseases from the newcomers. Some could not be bothered to go on hunting and fishing, and some died.

Then the jungle had to be cleared. Here there are special problems, as it is extremely hot, and rain is often very heavy. The machinery gets stuck in the mud, and people do not want to work for long in these conditions.

The new road opens up the jungle for development. Valuable minerals and oils have been discovered, and this means that even more jungle will be cleared.

Not only is the environment of this vast natural area changing. Clearing the jungle has other effects. As the number of people increases, so they produce more carbon dioxide. Plants take in carbon dioxide and give out oxygen. Cutting down all this jungle means that there are fewer trees and plants to produce oxygen. The Amazon Basin, as one of the largest natural areas, used to provide a "store" of oxygen for the world. There may be serious effects on the oxygen available for us.

Noise

Some countries seem to take the problem of noise pollution more seriously than Britain. Here the noise level is checked in a textile factory in Hungary, by staff of the Research Institute for Labour Safety. One man holds a special microphone, and the noise level is being measured in decibels on a noise meter held by the man in the front.

▼

About 2 million people in Britain today are working in an ENVIRONMENT where there are dangerous levels of NOISE. Hundreds of thousands of workers are completely or partially deaf due to the noise where they work. In September 1974 a company newspaper, the

"Lucas Combine News", reported:

> One Shop Stewards' committee reports that in a sheet metal workshop, the noise levels are so high that 40 of the 161 workers are deaf. In fact it is said that you can tell an experienced worker in that shop because he can lipread.

Noise has increased at work as industry has become more mechanized. It has also increased in our everyday life. Machines used at home — vacuum cleaners, washing machines, hairdryers — are all noisy. Cars, heavy lorries, buses, motorbikes and vans are also noisy. We get used to a high level of noise and do not realize that it may be making us deaf.

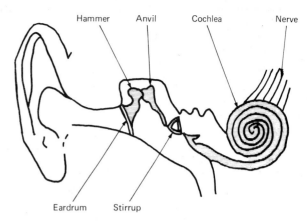

Look carefully at this diagram which shows the ear. When sound reaches it, the eardrum vibrates. The vibration is carried by the three tiny bones (called the hammer, anvil and stirrup — because of their shape) of the middle ear. The cochlea picks up the vibration. This is full of liquid which is set in motion by the sound. Thousands of tiny hair cells sense this motion, and send nerve messages to the brain, and so we hear sound.

WHAT IS NOISE?

Very simply, *noise is unwanted sound*. A sound that one person enjoys may be a noise to another person. To someone waking up in the morning after a good night's sleep, a bird singing may be a pleasant sound. To another person who has just got off to sleep after a very restless night, the same singing bird may be a noisy disturbance. The latest pop record may be a very pleasant sound, but to someone trying hard to concentrate on revision for important exams it could be a noise. Sound and noise are subjective. This is why it is sometimes difficult to understand why people complain about noise that you do not even realize is there.

HOW WE HEAR

Sound is carried through the air by SOUND WAVES. Sound waves are like the waves made when a stone is dropped in water. The waves are biggest where the stone is dropped, and gradually get smaller and smaller. Sound is loudest near to the source of the sound, and gradually gets quieter further away.

The sound waves make our eardrums vibrate. The eardrum vibrates very gently with a quiet sound. An extremely loud noise can make the eardrum vibrate so much that it breaks.

Deafness can be caused by wax in the ear — which stops sound from reaching the eardrum. An infection in the middle ear or other disease may also affect hearing. Lastly, a loud noise or a bang on the head may damage the eardrum or the bones in the middle ear. In nearly all cases of deafness caused by loud noise the hair cells and nerves in the inner ear are damaged.

SOUND INTENSITY AND FREQUENCY

INTENSITY is the amount of energy that the vibrating air particles carry to the eardrum. The range of intensity is very great — the quietest sound is about 10 million million times less intense than painful sound. The damage done to hearing increases with the intensity of sound.

Most noise is a mixture of FREQUENCIES. When a single tone sound is produced — like a note on a guitar or piano — the air particles vibrate back and forward a certain number of times per second. This is the frequency or pitch, and is measured in *cycles per second* or *hertz*(Hz). High frequencies cause more damage to hearing than low frequencies. They are often unpleasant as well — screeching brakes, a shriek squeaking chalk on the blackboard, all have high frequencies. As we get older, it is more difficult to hear high frequencies.

Because the range of sound intensity is so large — painful sound being 10 million million times more intense than the quietest sound — sound is measured on a logarithmic scale. The units on this scale are DECIBELS (dB). The logarithmic scale means, for example, that 70 dB is ten times (10x) the intensity of 60 dB. 60 dB is ten times (10x) the intensity of 50 dB. 70 dB is then 10 x 10 the intensity of 50 dB — that is 100 times the intensity.

dB Reading	
0	Silence.
10	Heartbeat and breathing can be heard.
20	Broadcasting Studio.
30	Very quiet. Whisper at 4.5 metres in quiet library.
40	Quiet conversation, as in a quiet office.
50	Living room in a normal home — everyday bustle.
60	A busy office – normal conversation.
70	Noisy children. Vacuum cleaner at 2.7 metres. Difficult to use telephone.
80	Phone at 1 metre.
90	Pneumatic drill at 9 metres. Underground railway platform. Hearing damaged after 8 hours per day. OFFICIAL "ACCEPTABLE" LEVEL.
100	Noisy factory. Woodsander. Shouting in ear.
110	Mechanical riveter. Shot-blasting.
120	Inside a disco. Jet take-off at 30 metres. Eardrums ring.
130	Pop group amplifier at 0.3 metre. Painful.
135	OFFICIAL MAXIMUM PERMITTED EXPOSURE.
140	Jet take-off at 24 metres. Temporary deafness.
160	303 rifle fired beside ear. Permanent deafness if noise continues for several minutes.
200	Moonrocket at 305 metres. Death.

The table shows examples of decibel readings from 0 to 200. Noise is measured on a noise or sound level meter. This can be a very simple machine, as small as a pocket calculator, or a large complicated device which can be set to measure different types of noise. The noise meter is pointed in the direction of the noise. A sensitive receiver picks up the noise which is registered by a needle on a scale, to give the dB reading. Ordinary noise meters cannot register sudden noises like a gun or car backfiring, and so special measuring equipment is used.

WHAT CAUSES NOISE?

If you ask people what noise they find most annoying, they are very likely to answer "traffic". People who live near a busy road or intersection are often disturbed by the roar of traffic. It was estimated that in 1980 29 million people were subjected to traffic noise of more than 70 dB for over two hours each day. An American medical researcher, Dr Louis Freeman, said: "If city noise continues to rise as it has been doing — which is at the rate of one or more decibels per year — everyone will be stone deaf by the year 2,000." There are more cars on the roads, and the number of cars is increasing. Although some people may be concerned about conserving oil, and reducing air pollution, not so many are worried about noise. People sit in cars, where the car engine is making noise, and listen to the radio or a cassette. The volume has to be turned up to hear this sound above the engine. Lorries are getting heavier, and the noise of this weight is bounced off the road. Normal conversation is impossible in some houses when a heavy lorry goes past.

Aeroplanes are another source of irritating noise. People who live near airports must often put up with noise levels of 90-100 dB when planes take off. Planes take off as often as one a minute in some busy airports. Studies done in primary schools near Heathrow Airport discovered that children found it very difficult to concentrate. Teachers could not talk for longer than two minutes at a time because the noise of the planes drowned their voices. The children got fed up with the continual interruptions and lost interest in the lesson.

Concorde flies at twice the speed of sound. The normal speed of sound in air at sea level is 336 metres per second, or about 1,200 kilometres per hour. When Concorde moves through the air faster than the speed of sound, or SUPERSONICALLY, it causes a disturbance called a SONIC BOOM. Air in front of the plane has no sound warning that it is coming. The plane slams into the air in its path and produces shock waves — these are sonic booms.

Some people believe that sonic booms are very dangerous. They do damage buildings, making them vibrate and cracking plaster. The sudden noise of sonic booms frightens animals — and some people. By 1982 Britain was still unable to fly Concorde to Australia because some countries inbetween would not allow it to fly supersonically in their air space.

The noise level has risen as industry has

Any plane flying faster than the speed of sound makes shock waves — or sonic booms. This diagram of the flight of a supersonic plane shows that anyone living in the area shaded will be affected by sonic booms. The "boom-path" is from 80 to 130 kilometres wide.

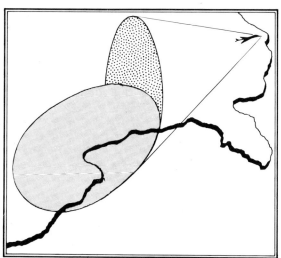

become more mechanized. Old machinery has been speeded up, and those who design new machinery do not usually pay great attention to the noise level. It often costs more money to insulate machinery than some manufacturers are prepared to pay. Industrial noise is one of the main causes of deafness. Workers are often supplied with ear-muffs to cut out some of the noise. These can be very hot to wear, and also prevent conversation between the workers. It is interesting to note that the maximum limit of 90 dB, as stated by the Factory Inspectorate's Code of Practice, is high enough to damage hearing.

The British Society for Social Responsibility in Science included in their booklet "Noise" seven questions that workers should ask themselves:

1. At work, do you have to shout to be heard by someone near you?
2. Is your hearing dulled just after your shift, or did you notice this when you started your noisy job?
3. Do you get head noises or ringing in the ears after work?
4. Have you or your family noticed that your hearing is getting any worse?
5. Do you have difficulty hearing people when others are talking as well? For example, at meetings or parties.
6. Do you ever get headaches or giddiness?
7. Do many of the older workers seem hard of hearing?

If the answer to any of these is yes, you are probably exposed to a dangerous noise level.

Building and repair work are often accompanied by irritating noise. The noise of a pneumatic drill, or of a pile driver, is INTERMITTENT NOISE. The noise is not CONSTANT; it comes and goes. This is more annoying than a steady noise, although it is not so dangerous. People who live near building sites or large road works have to put up with this sort of noise, as well as with a lot of dirt and dust, for a long time. Some

Industrial noise is one of the main causes of deafness. This is an advertisement for hearing protectors, so that workers' ears are protected from unwanted noise.

new building techniques have not helped. The first buildings in Thamesmead, a new town in South East London, were erected

Noise Induced Hearing Loss:
It does to speech what
frosted glass does to a face.

Imagine not clearly understanding a single word that's said to you. Ever again.

Yet that is what happens with Noise Induced Hearing Loss.

Just as distorted glass blurs vision, so Noise Induced Hearing Loss blurs sound. Particularly speech.

Any noisy work place can cause it. A special type of deafness brought about by the destruction of the hearing cells.

There is no cure.

And no escaping the appalling effects it can have on a man. The feeling of total isolation. Of being shut off from his family. Of living in fear of losing his job. Even though there's no cure there is a way to prevent it.

Bilsom Hearing Protectors. From communication muffs and ear defenders to hygienic disposable ear plugs. Designed to kill unwanted noise without killing conversation.

Which is why operators are happy to wear them.

Also because they're specially matched to meet and treat any disturbing level of noise in almost any kind of situation.

Above all, because they're comfortable.

Bilsom Hearing Protectors are now available in more and more companies throughout British industry. All you have to do is ask. Make today the day you do it. We'd hate our advice to fall on deaf ears.

Bilsom
In defence of hearing

Bilsom International Limited, 47a Bell Street, Henley-on-Thames, Oxfordshire RG9 2AH. Tel: (04912) 4288 or 6525.

on "piles", which had to be driven 7.5 metres into the ground by a noisy pile-driver. However, the CONSTANT NOISE of a dumper truck going backwards and forwards or of an electricity generator on a building site are disturbing.

Pete Townshend of "The Who" was reluctant to play in the 1979 Concerts because he was worried about his hearing. Many people who play in groups and bands have hearing problems, as a direct result of the level of the noise which the instruments produce. Some people at discos and concerts stand very close to the amplifiers. Their ears ring and they find it difficult to hear afterwards. Their hearing may be permanently damaged. Electric instruments, like guitars, can be connected to a machine called a "lighthouse", which makes different coloured lights flash on and off in time to the music. When the guitar produces sound above a certain dB level, the "lighthouse" cuts off the electricity supply. The music is interrupted, but musicians soon learn to play within the dB level — and their hearing, and that of the audience is not then affected.

Many homes now have electrical equipment such as washing machines, vacuum cleaners, food mixers, liquidizers, tumble dryers and dishwashers. Although machines are technically advanced — they may even contain their own microcomputer — not enough attention has been paid to the noise they produce. To be in a kitchen with a washing machine and tumble dryer switched on, using a food mixer, can be literally deafening.

The noise of a pneumatic drill or rammer used in road repair work is a source of irritation to many people, especially those living in nearby houses, when the road works continue for any length of time.

THE EFFECTS OF NOISE

Too much noise can cause temporary or permanent hearing loss. Temporary deafness is noticed when people first start a noisy job, or have been to a noisy disco. When people get used to the noise, then their deafness may become permanent. First of all, they cannot hear high and low sounds; everything gets fainter. They want the volume on the television or radio turned up more than everyone else. They say that other people are whispering — while they shout. Then they cannot hear "s" on the end of words; then fifteen and sixteen sound the same. Lastly, they cannot understand what someone is saying, even though they can see their lips moving.

Noise can also cause stress. This in turn can cause heart attacks and strokes. People who live near airports are eight times more likely to go to a mental hospital for treatment, than those living in a quiet area. Double vision and colour blindness result from too much noise as well. The vibration from heavy lorries makes buildings shake and also affects our body structure.

PREVENTING NOISE POLLUTION

It is possible for everyone to prevent noise from damaging their hearing — by wearing ear-protectors, ear-muffs or ear-plugs. This is inconvenient because it also cuts out sounds which we want to hear.

The British government has set noise limits for motor vehicles. Yet a recent survey showed that over 30% of heavy lorries were breaking this limit. The EEC wants to introduce laws to allow heavier lorries on to British roads. The noise level would also increase.

By-passes around towns take the noisy traffic away from where people live, but they cost a lot of money to build, and use up land needed for producing food.

Vertical take-off planes reduce noise levels a great deal. "Hush-kits" are available for fitting to noisy aircraft. Both use more fuel than conventional planes. Neither are used by many of the world's plane companies. People who live near airports can get government grants to help them double-glaze their windows. This cuts down the noise as long as the windows are shut.

It is possible for industry to reduce the noise of machinery. Adapting the machinery and lining walls with noise-absorbing materials both help. £100-worth of rubber mountings removed a dangerously loud noise in a new power press at the GKN works in Telford, for example.

Pressure from consumers could persuade manufacturers to produce domestic machines which are quieter.

Other countries have an official noise control department, which sets standards and advises the government. In Britain there is no such department. The Noise Abatement Society is a voluntary organization which aims to stop all unnecessary noise. Perhaps, since the noise level in Britain is increasing, and so many people are affected by it, there should now be an official department to control noise.

People living near airports not only have their lives disturbed when aeroplanes land or take off, but also have to put up with the rather alarming sight of the aeroplane flying just over their rooftops. This jumbo jet is approaching the runway at Heathrow.

Rivers

CLEANING UP THE YORKSHIRE RIVERS

At the beginning of 1972 the Yorkshire River Authority was in charge of more than 476 kilometres of rivers. Most of these were very POLLUTED, and were not improving. More than 70% of the EFFLUENT put into rivers was not treated in any way.

Geoffrey Lean wrote six articles about the rivers in a newspaper called the *Yorkshire Post* in April and May 1972. He named 25 firms and local authorities as the main polluters. The newspaper found that the Yorkshire River Authority was not able to do its work effectively because it did not have enough money. Also it did not use its power to prosecute.

The response from the public was tremendous. Local people looked at the levels of pollution themselves. They contacted their MPs and told them about the effects of the pollution. School pupils measured the oxygen in the water. Anglers rescued fish with diseases and treated them, when they could, in their own homes.

Within three weeks of these articles appearing in the paper, the River Authority started to clean up the river. They employed more people in the pollution prevention department. They gave them new offices and a laboratory which would deal with 20,000 samples of river water each year. (The old laboratory had dealt with only 4,000 samples each year.)

Within one year all the 25 firms and local authorities which had been named had taken action to clean up their discharges into the rivers.

In two years the River Authority had made 35 prosecutions on pollution charges.

OUR WATER SUPPLY

Water authorities get their water from two sources: ground water, where rain has seeped through the ground into the rocks, and surface water, which includes rivers, lakes and

The effects of pollution are often unpleasant. These fish were killed when the water was polluted.

RESERVOIRS. Before it goes into the mains water supply to our houses, water is usually treated, although it may be taken directly from the river if the quality is good enough. It is very important that the river water is not too contaminated. Most of the impurities can be removed even from badly polluted water, but this costs a lot of money.

At a waterworks, water to be treated is usually pumped to a storage RESERVOIR. Here, most of the suspended solids settle out. The water is then piped to the filter beds. These beds contain 1 metre of sand on a gravel base. The water is sprinkled over the top of the filter bed, where special bacteria act on the POLLUTANTS in the water and so remove the impurities. Any remaining contamination is killed by chlorine which is added.

The water authorities are responsible for making sure that the water supply is safe. They check it before, during and after treatment, before it goes into the water mains, and while it is in the mains. These checks are done very carefully, according to guidelines set out by the World Health Organization and by the government.

The last serious outbreak of disease caused by the water supply was in Croydon in 1937. If the water authority finds that the bacteria level is too high, it may increase the amount of chlorine which is added to the water. Sometimes it may cut off the supply of water. Or it may flush out the water mains to clean them.

RIVERS AND WASTE

Rivers can deal with WASTE. Leaves, dead fish and animals which are in the water or fall into the river gradually decay. They are attacked by organisms in the water which use oxygen to break them down. The problem occurs when too much waste is put into the water. The organisms use more and more oxygen to attack the waste, and there is none left for the fish and other river creatures. These die, but then there is not enough oxygen for the organisms to deal with them. At this stage other bacteria, which do not need oxygen, take over. These are called ANAEROBIC bacteria. They react on the waste, but produce unpleasant and smelly gases such as methane and hydrogen sulphide.

Given a chance, the river can recover. It can deal with things that will break down naturally, such as wood, leaves, paper, even sewage. These things are called BIODEGRADABLE. Other pollutants do not break down naturally — plastic, polythene, polystyrene, metals. These are called NONBIODEGRADABLE. Some of these also spoil the look of the river — plastic cups and plastic carrier bags caught up in the reeds on the bank of a stream are an EYESORE.

Other kinds of waste are more worrying. Some industrial waste discharged into our rivers can make serious problems for the water authorities, whose job it is to make sure that the water supply is fit for us to drink. Very small amounts of phenols (a group of chemicals) discharged into rivers react with

Swans look for food among old tyres, wood, mattresses and other rubbish. This sort of pollution is not only an eyesore, but can also be harmful to wildlife, as rusty nails and jagged metal and wires cause serious injury.

the chlorine which is used to purify the water. This gives the water a very unpleasant taste, which could occur in our drinking water.

The development of nuclear technology has meant that there is the possibility of water being contaminated by RADIOACTIVITY. Radioactive waste products from NUCLEAR POWER stations have leaked into the nearby water supply. The level of RADIATION in these rivers then became too high for safety, and the water could not be used. Very strict controls are needed in industries using nuclear technology.

The cheapest way for industry to get rid of waste is to dump it into the nearest river. That way, the industry does not have to pay for treating the waste, and pays only the cost of transporting the EFFLUENT to the river. Dangerous chemicals have been put into rivers, which have killed all the river life, and have been a hazard when the water has been pumped off for human use.

Industrial waste sometimes colours the river: orangey-red with iron compounds, green with some copper compounds, black near a coal washery. This may not do people much harm, but certainly does not look attractive. The water in the River Ebbw, for example, was orange from the discharge from the British Steel Corporation Works (now closed) at Ebbw Vale. The bed of the river is also covered with chemical deposits, and so there is hardly any fish or animal life in the river near the works.

Water authorities are now becoming much stricter about what is dumped into their rivers. The section at the beginning of this chapter shows what can be done when publicity highlights a bad example of pollution.

Sewage is another problem. Some areas do not treat their sewage very efficiently. This is most unpleasant for those who live near the OUTFALL, and the result is often no animal life or fish in the river. In 1970 an article in *The Times* featured the problem in Edinburgh. On a dry day 230 litres of sewage pour into the Firth of Forth from 9 pipes — from

GREATER LONDON COUNCIL
WARNING
OUTFALL APRON EXTENDS
160 FT FROM THE BOARD

The southern outfall of the Crossness Sewage Works on the River Thames. The treated liquid sewage is piped into the river. Although it is not harmful, a notice warns shipping. Notice the seagulls looking for food, and the sedimentation tanks in the background.

Cramond in the West to Joppa in the East — a distance of about 14 kilometres. When it has been raining, the sewage is diluted and up to 1,400 litres are discharged.

Water cools both the reactors in nuclear power stations and the fuel which is used in more conventional power stations. Water is usually piped in from the river, used as a cooling agent, and then returned at a higher temperature. The effect of this THERMAL POLLUTION is to change the ECOSYSTEM of the river. As well as this, the amount of oxygen in the river is reduced, so cutting down the river's ability to cope with waste.

By using good farming techniques and fertilizers, weed killers and insecticides, farms in Britain are very efficient. The problem is that the chemicals which aid that efficiency also pollute. They can be washed out of the soil and end up in rivers and lakes — these are called RUN-OFF POLLUTANTS. Insecticides and weed killers can kill the river life. Fertilizers may cause EUTROPHICATION. They "fertilize" the algae in lakes so that they multiply, using up the oxygen. The result is an area of water where there is no life apart from algae, looking like green paint. This has happened in Lake Geneva in Switzerland, and also in Lake Erie in America. It was estimated that in 1968 Lake Erie received 37,500 tonnes of nitrogen from run-off pollutants and 45,000 tonnes from sewage. Lakes do "age" naturally, but in the case of Lake Erie, the lake aged 15,000 years more quickly than if the pollutants had not been allowed to reach it.

People pollute rivers directly. They may use the river as a dump. In cities particularly, a river may be regarded as a convenient place to put unwanted mattresses, broken bicycles, old car tyres. The river becomes an EYESORE, and this bulky rubbish may block the flow of the river and contaminate the water. Oil from pleasure boats pollutes rivers which are used for recreation. Oil drained out of an engine is very difficult to get rid of, and some people pour this into a river. Some years ago many rivers were polluted by foam from detergents. Manufacturers were adding a foaming agent to their detergents, because people thought that a detergent was more efficient if there were a lot of bubbles. This caused tremendous problems for the SEWAGE TREATMENT plants. Some plants built expensive machinery to cope with the foam. Eventually, manufacturers were persuaded to reduce the foaming agent. With the increase

in automatic washing machines which use a low foaming detergent, this problem has decreased. However, phosphates are present in detergents, and these act in rivers in a similar way to fertilizers. They encourage the growth of algae, which reduce the level of oxygen in the water.

WATER SHORTAGE

The demand for water grows as the number of people increases, as industry uses more water, and as we use more water at home. During a rainy period it does not seem possible that we can ever be short of water in Britain, but this did happen in 1976. There was a severe DROUGHT. The use of hoses in gardens, automatic car-washers, and washing cars were all banned. People were encouraged to have showers instead of baths, or to bath in less water, put a brick into the lavatory cistern, and save as much water as they could. In some areas, people had their water turned off, and had to collect it from the nearest standpipe in the street. This was very inconvenient and hard work! On farms, people were even worse off. When their water supply ran dry, they had to collect their water and that for the animals, from pipes, sometimes a couple of kilometres away. RESERVOIRS were very low, and even rainmaking dances were held, to try to bring rain.

After this drought, the demand for water dropped, but it is now rising again. The problem is that most of the rain falls on the hills in the west of Britain. Here the rain has to be trapped in reservoirs and piped to where the people live. Building a new reservoir often means drowning people's homes and farms. Large areas of farm land are lost. In January 1980 a public inquiry opened in Whitehaven to look at plans to take water from Wast Water or Ennerdale Water in the Lake District. The lakes are in two of the most unspoilt areas of the Lake District. The proposals would mean building embankments, changing the route of the river, and flooding farms and

In 1976 there was a severe drought. This reservoir at Strinedale near Oldham is usually full. As the water level dropped due to lack of rain, the sides of the reservoir became exposed, and there was just a trickle of water flowing through the muddy bottom.

woodland. Many people object to losing their farms and homes, and spoiling areas of natural beauty.

There are fewer large towns in the western half of Britain. A lot of people live on the eastern side, where there is not enough rain to supply all the people. Waste water has to be treated and used again. People who live in London use water which has already been used at least twice before — in Oxford and Reading. But re-using water will not be enough. We shall still be short of water if we do not cut down on using water ourselves.

This leaflet was produced as part of the Water Savers ▶ Campaign after the 1976 drought, but most of the suggested ways of saving water can still apply now.

23

The River Thames

The River Thames is an example of an environmental success. It was always important for fish, but from 1810 onwards, fewer and fewer fish were caught. At that time lavatories were introduced in London. There was no proper SEWAGE TREATMENT system, and the waste flowed into cesspits. These often overflowed and caused much pollution to the river.

Thames Water Authority inspectors take regular ▶ samples of river water and all consented discharges, and keep in touch with the local authorities and industry on matters likely to affect the Authority's interests. In order to avoid delay with reports of pollution incidents, inspectors can be contacted by radio anywhere in the area. (The Thames Water Authority has powers under the Rivers (Prevention of Pollution) Acts to lay down consent conditions for any discharge of sewage and industrial effluent.)

◀ Anglers and angling clubs can get advice from the Thames Water fisheries staff. Fish surveys help to prevent disease, as well as deciding on stocking or destocking the rivers in the area.

Fish recorded at the West Thurrock Power Station, on the River Thames	1963	1964	1967	1968	1969	1974	1975	1976	1977	1978
Pollack										○
Rockling										○
Scaldfish										○
Sea Scorpion									○	
Butterfish									○	
Pipefish									○	
Bull Rout									○	
Mackerel									○	○
Rockling									○	○
Lemon Sole									○	○
Rockling								○	○	○
Weever								○	○	○
Sea Snail								○	○	○
Rockling							○			
Goby								○	○	○
Goby							○	○	○	○
Goby						○	○	○	○	○
Mullet						○	○	○	○	○
Sand Smelt						○	○		○	○
Lumpsucker						○	○		○	
Sea Bream						○				
Sand Eel						○	○	○	○	
Pilchard						○				
Trigger-fish						○				
Rockling						○				
Salmon						○				○
Pipefish						○			○	
Goby						○	○	○	○	○
Mullet						○	○	○	○	○
Red Mullet						○	○	○	○	○
Pipefish						○	○	○	○	○
Poor Cod						○	○	○	○	○
Dory						○	○	○	○	○
Shad							○	○		○
Haddock				○						
Gurnard				○		○	○	○	○	○
Lamprey			○	○						
Gurnard			○	○		○	○	○	○	○
Stickleback			○	○	○	○	○	○	○	○
Scad				○		○	○	○	○	○
Shad				○			○	○	○	○
Cod				○		○	○	○	○	○
Sand eel				○	○			○		○
Brill								○		
Anchovy					○	○	○	○		○
Smelt			○	○	○	○	○	○	○	○
Herring			○	○	○	○				○
Conger			○	○		○	○	○		○
Pipefish			○	○	○	○		○	○	○
Bib			○		○	○		○	○	○
Sand Eel						○		○		○
Bass			○	○	○	○	○	○	○	○
Goby			○	○	○	○	○	○	○	○
Dragonet			○	○	○		○	○	○	○
Gurnard			○	○	○	○	○	○	○	○
Pogge			○	○	○	○	○	○	○	○
Sea Snail			○	○	○	○	○	○	○	○
Plaice			○	○	○	○	○	○	○	○
Flounder			○	○	○	○	○	○	○	○
Sprat			○	○	○	○	○	○	○	○
Sole			○	○	○	○	○	○	○	○
Dab			○	○	○	○	○	○	○	○
Whiting			○	○	○	○	○	○	○	○
Tadpole-fish		○		○			○	○	○	○
Lampern		○	○		○		○	○	○	○
Eel	○	○	○	○		○	○	○	○	○
	1	3	21	26	27	35	40	41	50	53

An extract from a leaflet issued by Thames Water, ▶
"Nature and the Freshwater River Thames".

Riverside industries such as slaughter houses, breweries and tanneries all dumped their waste in the Thames.

From about 1920 the river became so polluted that there was no fish or marine life in the Thames, and this continued for 40 years.

In 1953 the London County Council started a scheme to clean up the Thames. It rebuilt and extended the sewage treatment works at Crossness and Beckton, as sewage was the main cause of pollution. The clean-up campaign took 20 years to complete, and the success of this can be seen in the chart.

97 different types of fish have been found in the River Thames — including 2 salmon. This is especially significant because salmon only swim in clean water.

Thames Water now concentrates on pollution control. It tests the water chemically, as well as noting the types of water life.

Nature and the Freshwater River Thames

The freshwater River Thames is one of the best known lengths of river in the world.

The 140 mile stretch from its source above Cricklade in Wiltshire down to Teddington to the west of London provides a wealth of recreational facilities.

Throughout the year and especially during the summer months, thousands of pleasure craft are afloat cruising, sailing, rowing and canoeing. Children and adults can be seen fishing along the bank.

Families out for the day or on holiday use the towpaths and fields to picnic, walk or sit and take in the scenery.

The river passes through some very well-known towns and areas — Oxford, Abingdon, Marlow, Maidenhead, Windsor and Runnymead, and is the venue for international events such as the Henley Regatta. Great houses, monuments and historic sites can be found throughout its length.

Less evident, but just as important, are the gifts Nature itself has given to the river — birds, fish and flowers. The freshwater Thames may not be so richly endowed as some other rivers in the country but what it has is there to be enjoyed by everyone.

The Sea

Oil pollution was not modern man's only gift to the sea. As we kept a lookout scarcely a day passed without some form of plastic container, beer can, bottle or more perishable materials such as packing-cases, cork and other rubbish, drifting close by Ra 2's side.

So wrote Thor Heyerdal, who sailed across the Atlantic Ocean in 1970 in a boat of reeds.

The sea covers 70% of the earth's surface. There are one thousand million cubic kilometres of water in the sea, and this dilutes most harmful WASTE which is put into it. Why should we be concerned about the effects of dumping rubbish in the oceans if they are so vast?

Most of the fish, sea creatures and plants live in the shallow part of the sea, around the land masses. It is here that most of the EFFLUENT is dumped, and it is here that most of the fish is caught. Fish form part of a FOOD CHAIN, and the end of that chain is often people, who eat the fish. To add the chemical DDT to the sea, in the proportion of one part DDT to a million parts sea water, would be enough to reduce the sea's oxygen production by 75%. The eventual result would be death — because the sea produces more than half of all the oxygen on earth.

THE RAINFALL CYCLE

All of our water supply comes from the sea. In the rainfall cycle, the sun shines on the sea and heats the water surface; the water turns into a colourless gas — water vapour. The water vapour rises and forms clouds, which are blown across the land by winds. Above the land there are changes in temperature which cause the water vapour to turn into liquid again. The liquid falls onto the land as rain — which forms streams and rivers. It may also soak into the rocks and collect underground, where the rock is POROUS. We get our water supply from rivers, lakes, and underground wells.

THE SEA AS A RESOURCE

The sea supplies not only our water, but also food in the form of fish. Most of the fish are caught in the coastal areas, as the table shows.

Area	% of Ocean	Area (sq km)	Annual Fish Production (tonnes)
Open Ocean	90	326,000,000	1,609,000
Coastal Zone	9.9	36,000,000	120,000,000
*Coastal Up-Welling Areas	0.1	360,000	120,000,000

* These are areas where there are strong movements of water. This brings minerals to the surface, and so attracts PLANKTON. Plankton in turn attract fish.

Some people seem to think that the fish in the sea are just there to be caught, and that, when there is not enough food produced on land, the sea can be harvested. In fact, this is not the case. As the table shows, the greater part of the ocean — the open ocean — does not yield much fish. Already parts of our seas are OVER-FISHED. In the 1960s, Peru, in South America, was the major supplier of anchovies. These are small fish, belonging to the herring family, which can be made easily into fishmeal. Fishing anchovies off the coast of Peru was the world's largest ocean harvest of a single species. Unfortunately, too many fish were caught, and the anchovies were not able to reproduce in enough quantities. Now, fishmeal production has slumped dramatically in Peru.

A similar situation has resulted with herring fishing in the North Sea. Today, the only stock of herring left in European waters is off the west coast of Scotland. In season, over 300 ships fish there. They suck up the herring into the holds of the boat, using large "vacuum cleaners", and so they can catch what was once a week's quota of fish in a couple of days. Already the fisheries in Iceland and Norway have been killed off. Yields in the North Sea dropped by 300% between the 1960s and 1980. The EEC is working on a fisheries policy. But action is needed now to control net sizes — so that young fish are not caught — and to limit the total amount of fish which may be caught from the area.

Whaling is another example of exploitation. Whales have been used in the manufacture of many different things: candles, soap, perfumes, bones for corsets, brushes, fertilizers, jellies, medicine, "leather", cosmetics, tennis racket strings, surgical stitches, pet foods, dynamite, soups, margarine, wax crayons. They were too useful for their own good. By the nineteenth century some species had almost disappeared. In the 1940s the biggest whales — the blue whale — became scarce. The whalers then started to kill fin whales. When fin whales declined, they fished for Seis, and now the sperm whale. With modern techniques, and FACTORY SHIPS, hunting whales does not give the whale much of a chance. The barbed harpoon weighs 73 kg, and explodes inside the whale. Dying often takes half an hour,

The International Whaling Commission met in Brighton in July 1980. Anti-Whaling demonstrators used an inflated "whale" to put their point across.

and can be as long as two hours. 85% of the whales killed are caught by Japan and Russia. Other countries, which do not actually hunt whales, are nonetheless at fault, because they encourage whale-hunting. For example, they import whale meat — mainly used for pet food — and other whale products. There have been a number of conferences to try to limit the number of whales caught, or even to stop the killing of whales altogether. The "Greenpeace" organization took a boat to the whaling grounds to try to prevent the whales from being caught. It is known that whales can send complex messages to each other. It would be a shame if it was not possible to carry out further research, because there were no longer any whales.

The sea provides us with water in the rainfall cycle, but in desert areas, there is not enough rainfall — less than 250mm per year. DESALINATION PLANTS have been built to provide some of these areas with more water. Sea water is heated; water vapour is produced; this is cooled, and is fresh water; the salts remain behind. The first desalination plants were expensive, but they are now much cheaper. In Jersey, in the Channel Islands, for example, a desalination plant has been found to be cheaper and more efficient than building a new RESERVOIR.

As well as food and water, the sea can provide energy. Scientists are looking at power from the waves or the tide. In Brittany, in northern France, a tidal station has been built. A dam has been built across the River Rance where it enters the sea. At high tide, gates on the dam are opened and sea water flows in. The gates are then shut, and the height of water held in the dam is used to make electricity — in the same way as in a conventional HYDRO-ELECTRIC POWER station. The area is popular for sailing, and special efforts were made so that boats could have access to the river. Locks were built into the dam for them to get to the sea. Calculations show that, to get the same amount of energy as from one tonne of coal, one tonne of sea water has to

fall 3 kilometres. On this basis, wave power seems uneconomic and will probably not be used unless conditions are ideal. Floating power stations, with wave-powered paddles to drive water turbines to make power, seem more likely. Clearly there is still some research to be done, but this does seem a possible future power source.

Lastly, the sea is a source of oil and minerals which have been found in the rocks under the water. Sometimes it is too difficult and dangerous to mine for these. Oil is in such demand that it is worth building expensive drilling rigs to go deep down to get it. North Sea oil has helped Britain's economy, as it has been possible to sell it abroad.

HOW THE SEA IS POLLUTED

When the *Torrey Canyon* went aground in March 1967, carrying over 100,000 tonnes of oil, more than 10,000 birds were killed as a result. Seabirds spend much of their time diving into the water for food. When oil gets on their feathers, they preen to try to remove it. The oil is swallowed, and the bird is poisoned. Oil also destroys the natural waterproofing of the feathers, and so the bird becomes wet and cold, and may die. These birds often come on to the shore, to try to dry out. On the shore, they may die of starvation, because the oil on their feathers stops them from moving easily to find food. The Royal Society for the Protection of Birds learnt much from the deaths of the 10,000 birds after the *Torrey Canyon* disaster. They found that a special cleaning agent had to be used to completely remove the oil. The birds could not be set free until their feathers had become waterproof again. Even still, many birds died from shock.

The *Torrey Canyon* was the first big oil tanker disaster to affect our coast. It killed seabirds and many sea creatures and plants. The oil was washed up around the shore as a thick, sticky brown mess. This is the "tar" that gets on clothes and shoes on the beach.

In 1967 the 61,000-tonne tanker, *Torrey Canyon*, hit the Seven Stones Reef, and the oil slick which was the result can be seen in this photograph.

Oil is washed ashore as a brown sticky mess. It was very difficult to clear it up from this beach because ▶ of the pebbles. Once oil gets onto the feathers of a bird, its chances of survival are very small.

It was so deep in places that it could be shovelled off the beach. It was not too difficult to remove the oil from a flat sandy beach. The problem was much worse on a pebbly beach, or around a rocky coastline. Special detergents were used to try to remove the oil. These detergents also killed most of the things living on the beach.

It is easier to deal with an OIL SLICK at sea, before it reaches the coast. The oil can be contained within a certain area, with a floating boom, and then sucked up from the surface of the sea. Or the oil can be absorbed on nylon "fur" laid on the water, and then squeezed out. If detergents are used at sea, they make the oil sink to the bottom and so affect the sea life there.

Oil gets into the sea from oil tankers. The *Torrey Canyon* in 1967 and the *Amoco Cadiz* in 1979 ran aground in shallow water. Sometimes oil is spilled accidentally. Too often, oil gets pumped back into the sea with the sea water which is used by ships to wash out their oil tanks. There are laws to stop this, but it is very difficult to find out which ship has been at fault when the oil is washed up on shore.

In the early 1970s it was estimated that anyone who swam in the Mediterranean in the summer had a one-in-seven chance of getting a disease from viruses. This was due to the untreated sewage in the sea. The Hague, in the Netherlands, dumps untreated sewage into the sea. Unfortunately, the tide and winds wash the solids back onto the beaches.

A number of coastal towns pipe untreated sewage into the sea — in Britain as well as in Europe. The sewage should be treated first, by being sieved so that the lumps are broken up. The pipes should go down into the sea at least 350 metres beyond low water. In these cases, the sea can treat the sewage. Even

The Cockenzie Power Station, East Lothian, Scotland. Some power stations, like this one, use sea water to cool the heating fuel. The water is put back into the sea 10° hotter. This affects the oxygen supply in the water, as well as the sea life.

if there are freak winds and tides, the sewage is not harmful or unpleasant if washed near the coast. A report in *Which?* magazine in 1975 found that almost 200 OUTFALLS around England and Wales were unsatisfactory.

The sea and coast are used as a dump by many industries. Many of the beaches in Northumberland and Durham have been ruined by coal-waste. In Cornwall, the waste from the china-clay pits is dumped off the coast, near St Austell. 200,000 tons of nerve and mustard gas, stored in metal containers, were dumped 200 miles off the west coast of Scotland after the last war. At Windscale in Cumberland, RADIO-ACTIVE EFFLUENT is pumped into the North Sea less than 2.5 kilometres from the shore.

For years the Chisso Chemical Company dumped their waste into the sea at Minimata Bay in Japan. This waste contained mercury. In 1953 the first sign that there was anything wrong was when the cats in the area began to get ill and die. Seventy-eight people died, too. Babies were born terribly deformed, blind, deaf, paralysed, and mentally retarded. It was traced back to the mercury in the fish caught in Minimata Bay. Mercury attacks the brain and the body, and eventually kills. The disease is called MINIMATA DISEASE.

```
┌─ PREVENTING POLLUTION OF THE SEA ─┐
```

The real problem about sea pollution is that the pollution is absorbed by sea creatures, including fish. Fish form part of a FOOD CHAIN, and people are at the end of that chain. Dumping EFFLUENT or WASTE into the sea may be cheap and easy, but, as in the case of Minimata Disease, the results may be horrific.

There are laws which should prevent oil pollution apart from accidental spillage. It is not easy to identify which ship has contravened them. Some ships are registered in countries which do not recognize international agreements. These ships are said to "sail under a flag of convenience". In fact, this is a major problem with sea pollution. Large areas of the sea do not "belong" to anyone. Some countries feel that they have a right to dump their dangerous waste in the sea because no one country has the authority to tell them to stop. In 1972 Iceland increased its territorial waters (the amount of sea around the coast belonging to the country) from 19 km to 80 km. This made problems for Britain, which fished for cod off the Icelandic coast, and a "cod war" began. There have been meetings between countries to try to divide up the sea — but no satisfactory solutions.

The National Environment Research Council published a Coastal Code, which it suggests we bear in mind, "so that we can all enjoy our natural inheritance and leave it unspoiled for others":

DO NOT subject easily damaged habitats (e.g. saltmarshes, sand dunes and cliff tops) to unnecessary trampling.

DO NOT move rocks unnecessarily, as some of the most delicate and susceptible forms of marine life occur on the undersides of stable rocks and boulders.

DO NOT frighten seals, seabirds or saltmarsh waders as this can affect their breeding cycles and expose their young to predators.

DO NOT spearfish in areas of special interest to conservationists or in the vicinity of other water users. Excessive spearfishing in limited areas can make fish shy and deplete some species.

DO NOT spill detergents, paint, solvents or fuel from boats as these can kill marine life.

MODERATE YOUR SPEED — The wash from a fast boat can destroy saltmarsh banks and swamp nests in estuaries.

SPREAD THE AREA FROM WHICH YOU COLLECT BAIT — Bait digging by anglers in limited areas can disturb the local fauna. Always back fill holes as these may be a danger to others.

The Countryside

FARMING

. . . every human being is now subjected to contact with dangerous chemicals . . . . In less than two decades of their use, the synthetic pesticides have been so thoroughly distributed . . . that they occur virtually everywhere . . . . These chemicals are now stored in the bodies of the vast majority of human beings, regardless of age. They occur in the mother's milk, and probably in the tissues of the unborn child.

(From *Silent Spring* by Rachel Carson)

A field of wheat is being sprayed with sulphate of ammonia from an aeroplane.

New technology has helped farmers a great deal. More efficient machines make the heavy and routine work of ploughing, sowing and harvesting much easier. Animals stay healthy because of modern medicines, and are fed more economically on carefully manufactured food. More crops are produced per hectare of land because chemicals have killed off the diseases and pests and improved the soil and plants. New strains of plants have been developed which also increase the yield. All this is part of the GREEN REVOLUTION — or high-yield agriculture. Producing more food is most important as the population increases. If farmers do not produce more, then there will be less food to go round and we could eventually starve.

Unfortunately, the Green Revolution is not without its hazards. Rachel Carson explains the problem of synthetic pesticides in her book *Silent Spring*, about the effect of chemicals on the countryside. One of the most important pesticides is DDT (Dichlorodiphenyltrichloroethane). This was discovered during the Second World War, and it destroys almost every harmful insect. DDT was used to kill the insects which carry the diseases of malaria, as well as yellow fever and typhus, in hot countries. In India, the number of malaria cases dropped from 75 million to 5 million in just 10 years, because of DDT. This chemical has saved millions of lives.

In the early 1960s mosquitoes and other insects were found which were immune to DDT. There was also a drop in the numbers of fish and sea birds. It was realized that DDT had been washed off the land into rivers and then into the sea. Here it had collected in bodies of PLANKTON — tiny sea creatures — which form part of a FOOD CHAIN. Eventually, sea birds which had fed on the plankton were laying infertile eggs. Others were laying eggs with such thin shells that the eggs broke before hatching. In Bolivia, in South America, using too much DDT killed most of the cats. As a result, there were more and more mice which carried black typhus. Many people died.

The World Health Organization says that the safe level of DDT in people is 0.01 milligrams per body kilogram a day. Some countries have restricted the use of DDT, and others, like Sweden and Denmark, have banned it altogether.

Insecticides (for killing insects), herbicides (for killing weeds), and fungicides (for killing fungus diseases) all affect the soil. These chemicals may be sprayed onto plants, but they are washed into the soil very quickly by the rain. Here they kill insects, organisms and bacteria in the soil. Soil copes naturally with dead plants and changes them into plant food. The chemicals may change the structure of the soil, and the rate at which it can turn the dead plants into plant food. Eventually, a good soil may become poor, or even infertile. The yield of crops will go down, and even more chemicals may then be used to improve the soil.

These chemicals also cause problems when they are washed by rainwater into rivers and lakes. Insecticides can kill the river creatures and eventually the fish. Fertilizers, which make plants grow better, also affect the growth rate of river plants, causing EUTROPHICATION. This is where algae use up all the oxygen in the water; and the water looks like green paint. (See page 22).

The chemical industry is looking at the problem of synthetic pesticides. It is trying to develop chemicals which do not have these bad effects, and may even break down into harmless substances. There are stricter laws now to control what goes into pesticides, and how they are used. Also, other methods of controlling pests are being used. Ladybirds from Australia were introduced into California to eat scale insects which attacked the orange and lemon trees. Ways of making the male or female insect infertile are also being investigated.

Hedges take up a lot of land around the edges of fields. Some of the hedges are very old — perhaps over 1,000 years old. Others

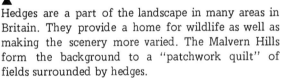

Hedges are a part of the landscape in many areas in Britain. They provide a home for wildlife as well as making the scenery more varied. The Malvern Hills form the background to a "patchwork quilt" of fields surrounded by hedges.

are newer — dating from the seventeenth and eighteenth centuries. It was at that time that the large, open fields were enclosed. Taking, or "grubbing" out hedges seems to have advantages: it releases land for farming; it also creates bigger fields, in which it is easier to use large machinery. Spraying pesticides is difficult in small fields, as the hedges must be avoided.

However, hedges are necessary too. They form a barrier to the wind, and protect crops. If there are no hedges, then the wind can blow the loose soil away. This happens in the Fens during a "Fen Blow", when the soil is blown away by the wind. It also happened in the 1930s in the United States. Most of the topsoil was blown away in Kansas and Oklahoma. The soil in the wind got into people's eyes and noses, and they wore masks to try to keep it out. When the wind finally dropped, many people found that there was no fertile soil on their farms. The area was called a "Dustbowl". The same effect can occur if too many hedges are grubbed.

Hedges provide a home for a great variety of wildlife. Animals, insects and plants all flourish in this shelter. Removing hedges removes what survives of our country wildlife.

Farmers are expected to produce food

◀ Battery chickens are kept in small wire cages. Food and water is on a tray in the front, and the eggs roll down to the wire rack at the front, so that they can be collected easily.

more efficiently. Sometimes the methods that they use in FACTORY FARMING, to meet the demand for produce, do not seem the best for the animals. To produce the number of eggs we use, chickens are kept in wire cages. The cages are small, to stop the chickens turning round. Their food and water are on a tray at the front end of the cage, and the eggs they lay are caught on a rack at the back and roll down to the front. The cages are usually placed in large barns or in specially built sheds. The temperature and light are carefully controlled to provide the best conditions for the hens to lay. It is quick and easy for the farmer to feed the chickens and collect the eggs. Although the cages, building and heating will cost money, most farmers prefer to keep chickens like this than to let them run around.

Free-range chickens are kept in an open area surrounded by wire. Their food is either put out in dishes or scattered on the ground. At night they have to be shut up in chicken houses; otherwise they may be attacked by foxes. Their eggs have to be collected; and may be laid anywhere in the chicken runs. It takes time to look after free-range chickens. Their eggs are usually more expensive, but some people prefer to pay the extra money. They think that the eggs taste better, and the chickens are healthier.

Other animals, like calves and pigs, may be kept in small pens. It is easier for the farmer to look after them when the food need only be poured into a trough at one end. Veal calves are kept in special conditions where the light is controlled. This makes their meat white.

Some people feel that it is wrong to coop up animals in this way. The animals should be free to move, at least to turn round. Farmers argue that it is simpler to look after animals

like this. They are in controlled heat and light which is better than being in a cold, wet field. It makes the food they produce cheaper too.

MEAT VERSUS VEGETABLES

On one acre of land enough protein can be produced for one person for:

2,224 days — growing soya beans
  887 days — growing wheat
  354 days — growing corn (maize)
   77 days — raising cattle for beef.

Five acres are needed to get enough protein from beef for one person for one year. Thirty people would have the same amount of protein each if soya beans were grown on those acres.

Raising animals is a very inefficient way of getting food from the land. Beef, pork and lamb may be very tasty, but if we were to eat grains, beans, and root vegetables instead, this would mean that the land could be used more economically. In Britain, about half our protein comes from meat. Other countries which have a large population, like Japan and China, eat very little meat. In the future we may have to consider eating less meat than we do now.

PROBLEMS IN THE COUNTRYSIDE

The countryside is not just land used for farming. More and more people are spending their free time in the country. They may just drive into the country at the weekend, to get away from the noise and bustle of the town. Or they may take part in a country activity, such as sailing, walking, rock-climbing or nature study.

The pressures on the countryside as more people use it appear in different ways. So many people are using well-known walks, like the Pennine Way, that these may have to be closed for some time each year, to allow the grassy paths to recover. It has even been suggested that synthetic grass or tarmac be laid, to protect the path.

Many people go to the country or the coast for a holiday. They may take a caravan with them, or rent one. A caravan holiday is different, interesting, and usually cheap. When caravan sites are carefully planned and landscaped, they do not cause a problem. When the caravans are parked as they are in the photograph of Porthcawl, they are an EYESORE.

Most of the land in towns has already been built on, and so new towns, new estates and new factories are often built in the country. Land which could be used to produce food is sold for building. The demand for land for building is so great that land fetches a better price when sold for development, than when it is sold for farming. Next, roads are needed, so that people can get to the houses or factories, and so more land is used. It is difficult to keep a balance between people's need for food and people's need for somewhere to live and work.

Supplying water to towns is another pressure on the countryside. Most rain falls on the west of Great Britain; most people live in the Midlands or the east. To provide enough water, dams are built, and large areas of land are flooded. This is explained on page 22. Many people object to losing homes, farms, and valuable farmland, even though they know that the water is needed. When a natural lake is used for water supply, there are sometimes restrictions about swimming or boating in it. Special pipes and embankments may have to be built around the natural lake as well — spoiling its beauty.

Some people think that caravans ruin stretches of beautiful countryside. It is easy to see why in this picture of Porthcawl, Wales.

Coniferous trees are planted as saplings, sometimes only 30 centimetres high. They grow into trees which can be used in 20 years. Special equipment has to be used to prepare the ground, which is often marshy. New roads are built as well. The landscape changes from desolate moorland to dark green forests. The ECOSYSTEM and so the wildlife of the moorland changes to that of a coniferous forest. Some people think that the changes are for

Map of National Parks and areas of outstanding beauty.
▼

On the Pennine Way people's boots have worn away the grass, and made muddy patches. To avoid the mud, people have walked on the grass on either side of the path, and it has become even wider and more worn.

The Forestry Commission has bought a lot of land in the Uplands of Britain on which to grow trees. Some of this is land which has been used for sheep-farming in the summer. Most of it is wild moorland which has a variety of wildlife. We need trees to supply us with paper. Growing our own trees means that we do not have to import so much wood, and so it saves the country money. The best trees to grow are those which mature quickly, and are softwoods. Softwoods can be made into pulp, and so into paper, more easily.

the worse. The natural wildlife changes, so does the soil. It becomes more acid because of the pine needles from the trees. Minerals are washed, or "leached", through the soil by the weak acid. The Forestry Commission believes that these changes are not important. Anyway, the land is being used to produce something that we need.

NATIONAL PARKS

In 1949 the government set up the National Parks Commission (renamed later the Countryside Commission). The aim was to preserve the natural beauty of certain chosen areas of the countryside — the National Parks. It was also hoped to encourage the public to enjoy these areas. Ten National Parks were made, as shown on the map on page 37. Most of the land in these parks is privately owned, but the owners must get special permission to make any alterations to buildings or to the use of land. The Parks are run by committees which are set up by the local authority and the government. The hope is that some of the pressures on the countryside can be controlled by protecting these areas.

Even the National Parks are not completely safe from development, however. In 1971 permission was given to the Rio Tinto Mining Company to make test drillings in Snowdonia. They were drilling for gold and copper. There are other pressures, too — water supply, building new roads, houses, and sometimes even factories.

The problem with the National Parks is that they are *too* successful. People have more leisure time now, and many people have cars. Motorways have brought the National Parks within a few hours' drive for most. All this means that families enjoy the isolation and beauty of the National Parks without realizing that, just by visiting them, they make the parks become less isolated, and their car and perhaps caravan destroy the beauty for other people.

The management of the parks — getting people to use them without ruining their character — is now a specialized job. Drivers are encouraged to leave their cars at specially landscaped car parks. There is often an Information Centre in the car park, and there may even be a free minibus to take people further on into the National Park. Here there are signposted walks, directions to sites of interest as well as sites of Special Scientific Interest (SSIs) and views, nature trails and picnic areas. Often those places where people can bathe, picnic and use boats are nearest the edges of the Park. This means that the centre is left for those who enjoy the isolation and the rugged scenery. The emphasis is on persuasive management — encouraging people to use the National Parks sensibly.

The conflict between keeping beautiful areas of countryside as they are, and developing any valuable resources they may contain is shown in this selection of newspaper articles.

Towns

When people started to live in towns, many of their problems began. Food had to be brought in, because it was impossible to grow enough crops and keep many animals within the town. Transport brought the food, and people to trade in the town, and often blocked the roads. Getting enough water was also a problem. Wells, pumps and rivers provided water, but even in Roman times water had to be piped to some towns. Getting rid of rubbish was a major difficulty. In Medieval times, WASTE was thrown into the street. People had to walk very carefully to avoid the rotting rubbish on the road, and that thrown out of upstairs windows. Towns were noisy, dirty and smelly, often full of disease and unhygienic.

People had been allowed to put up houses and shops wherever they owned land. There were few laws and restrictions, and the growth of towns was haphazard. The town council rarely thought of having a plan for the future growth and development of their town.

There were, and still are, many advantages to living in towns. There are more shops, and so a greater variety and choice of things to buy. There are usually more jobs in towns, which often pay higher wages. People go to the towns for entertainment. In the past, this would be guild plays and the travelling theatre. Now, most towns have a cinema, dance hall or disco, and sports facilities. Just seeing a lot of people or meeting friends in the town centre can be entertaining.

As more and more people live in towns, and the towns get bigger, so the problems increase. The large number of shops in town centres attract many people, who need transport to get there. Public transport is often inadequate, and the number of cars bringing people to the centre first of all cause congestion, and then need car-parking space. Lorries delivering goods to the shops also block roads, frequently in the morning rush hour. The pattern of employment is changing. Industries which attracted people to some towns in the first place may close when they cannot sell their goods. Sometimes the factories may move to other areas a long way away, where conditions are better. Either way, the workers may become unemployed, and find it difficult to get another job. They may not want to move when they have roots in a particular town.

During the last war (1939-45) many of our large towns were bombed, and when these bombed areas were cleared they could be developed. This provided a unique opportunity for planning within towns, and much thought was given to what towns *should* be like. Rather than a mix of houses, shops and industries, planners thought carefully about zones and areas. Most people go to towns to

New Towns.

shop, and shops formed the central zone or area. Entertainments, business, factories and offices, housing, sports centres and schools could all be built in the most convenient places.

_____ NEW TOWNS _____

Just after the war, as the population grew, there was a great demand for new houses, too. Rather than tinkering with established towns, the government decided to build new towns away from the large urban centres. They could be designed carefully, including all the up-to-date ideas of architects and town planners. However, even their ideas did not always keep pace with the rise in the standard of living. At Harlow New Town it was assumed that only one in ten households would have a car and so need a garage. Before Harlow was half-built, the plans had to be altered so that every other house had a garage. New towns were not just built after the last world war, however. Some "new" towns are much older. Letchworth (in 1908) and Welwyn Garden City (in 1919) were built at the beginning of this century. All new towns, though, were planned, and had areas or zones given over to one specific use.

The hopes and ideals of the government and town planners for these new towns did not always work out. The new towns were built away from the old centres. The planners hoped that this would encourage people to make a new community, rather than looking back to the old town. But people still had friends and relatives they wanted to visit in the old town, and they found the long journey, often by public transport, inconvenient. The most up-to-date house is not always home, and although the houses in new towns were very well-equipped, many people had problems settling in. Community Centres were built and residents' associations were formed to help.

In recent years the attraction of the new towns — the offer of a job — has also declined. When times are hard, people do not buy luxuries, and many of the factories in new towns make electrical goods like irons, toasters, food mixers, as well as similar "luxury" goods. When these factories close, unemployment affects new towns in a hard way. Despite all these problems, many people would agree that it is far better to live in a modern, comfortable house, in a pleasant and planned new town, than in a cold and damp slum.

_____ URBAN RENEWAL _____

Today, there is less emphasis on new towns, and more on looking at the centres of our older, established towns and cities.

Shops
To most people, shops indicate a town's importance. If there is a variety of big, well-

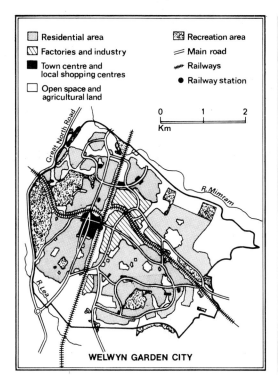

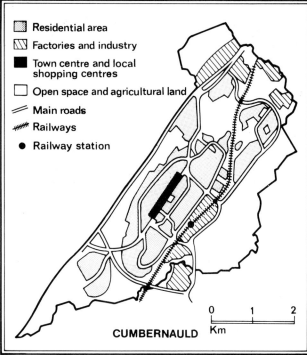

Look carefully at these plans of Welwyn Garden City and Cumbernauld (designated in 1956), and note how the residential areas (housing) are separate from the factories and industry. There is a main town centre as well as local shopping and neighbourhood centres.

known shops, then the town is a large one. Shops are usually sited at the centre of the town, and trading — buying and selling — was often the main reason why towns grew and became important. Nowadays, the shops in our towns have changed from just ten or twenty years ago. In 1947 there were only ten self-service stores in the whole of Britain. Most large department stores in towns are now self-service, with only a few counters, such as cosmetics and fabrics still having assisted service. Large picture windows show off artistic displays of the goods on sale. Music and announcements of particular bargains are broadcast throughout the store. Some town centres have been changed by the creation of pedestrian precincts, and all traffic is banned from the main shopping streets. Other towns have knocked down large areas in the centre to make shopping precincts. One

of the largest of these is in Croydon. Some people regret these changes, saying that towns have lost their character and individuality. Others are pleased with the choice they have and the variety of modern shops.

Housing

The state of housing in towns is a very big problem — for the people who live in the houses and for the planners. Many of the houses in our towns are over 100 years old. They were built when Britain was an important industrial nation, and when most people walked to work.

Woolwich, in London, has a great number of small Victorian houses. These were built when industry changed the village into an important town. There had been a dockyard at Woolwich since the time of Henry VIII. As Britain grew as an Empire, more ships were needed to carry manufactured goods out to the colonies, and to bring back raw materials. Ships also carried troops who went out to protect the colonies. Next to the dockyard at Woolwich, by the River Thames, was

41

This shopping precinct in Worthing looks a very attractive place to shop, as well as sit and rest. All traffic is banned, including bicycles — you can see them "parked" at the bottom of the picture.

a heath. At first, this was used to test the guns and military equipment. Soon a proper arsenal was built where the armaments were manufactured. Both the dockyard and arsenal attracted other industries — rope making, ship outfitting, ship repairing — and the army came to Woolwich as well. All needed workers. At this time there was no public transport, and certainly no cars. The workers' houses had to be built near enough to the industry for people to walk to work. These houses were built very close together on the slopes running back from the river. The houses are small, sometimes only four rooms, with a lean-to at the back for a scullery. At the time they were just what people needed. Now the houses are wearing out. Some do not have bathrooms or proper kitchens, as people expect. The dockyard and arsenal have long since closed.

In many towns the state of old houses like these is the same. The brickwork is crumbling, the woodwork needs replacing, and there may be no proper bathroom or kitchen. The roof may need re-tiling or re-slating, and there may

be rising damp. The local authority has to choose between renovating the houses and knocking them down to build new ones. It is usually cheaper to renovate — repair the roof, repoint the bricks, replace the woodwork, put in a new damp course, rewire and replumb the house, and possibly build an extension on the back for a new bathroom and kitchen. Sometimes, though, the houses are not worth repairing. If the houses are to be knocked down, then the people in them have to be rehoused until the new ones are built.

Some people may not want to leave their homes, even if they are in a bad state. They, and their parents before them, may have lived in that house all their lives. The houses may not have the facilities that we expect in modern houses, but often they have been well maintained, and people have put a lot of money and effort into their home. A close community spirit builds up in some roads. Neighbours look after each other. The younger ones keep an eye on old age pensioners and may collect their pension for them, and in return, the older people may baby-sit. Such friends and neighbours may be lost when the community is rehoused. On the other hand, some people cannot wait to get out of their house. It is cold, damp and a problem to maintain, and they look forward to a modern house, maisonette or flat.

New towns and new estates are usually built with a mixture of housing — flats, maisonettes and houses. In the 1950s many large blocks of flats were built. It was cheaper to build homes one on top of the other in this way, less land was needed, and a "factory" type of construction could be used. Panels were made in factories, which were moved to the site and assembled there. Some panels had windows, some had doors, and some contained the services, such as water supply, sewage pipes and the heating ducts.

Architects tried many different ways of making people feel at home in the flats. They included laundry and playrooms in the blocks, play areas in the grounds of the flats,

"streets in the sky" — where a corridor outside the front door was like a narrow ordinary street. Despite all this, some people found, and still find, living in flats difficult. Families with young children feel cut-off. Children cannot be supervised easily when they are playing outside. And play areas are too far from top-floor flats for parents to be able to keep an eye on them there. It is easier to keep the children indoors, but then they get bored and noisy. Older children are also bored, and may make their own excitement by vandali-

Numbers 25 and 26 Albert Road, Woolwich, 1899. These houses were built to house the workers at the Dockyard and Arsenal. They are small, and did not have the conveniences we expect in houses today. At the time they were just what the people needed.

In Pin Green, Stevenage, care has been taken to separate people from traffic. People living in the town houses on the left get to their local shops by walking under the road.

zing the lift and communal areas, and annoying neighbours. Pensioners can feel cut-off in blocks of flats, too, especially if the lift does not work, and there are many flights of stairs to climb. All in all, there are a number of problems about living in blocks of flats, or tower blocks. Some local authorities have had difficulties in moving people into tower blocks. And some blocks have been pulled down, even though they were only about fifteen years old. Many people, however, prefer living in a modern flat to a damp, dark house with few up-to-date amenities.

The modern houses replacing the rows of terrace houses built in the nineteenth century are carefully designed. Because of the land shortage in cities, as many houses as possible must be built in the area allowed. They must also be built as economically as possible. The local authority will be using ratepayers' and government money, and so will be working to a budget. If it is a private housing estate, the builder will not want to make the houses too expensive — otherwise people will not be able to afford them. Unfortunately, to save on cost, modern houses are not always well insulated for noise. Neighbours may be able to hear almost everything going on in the rooms next door, and the strain of living like this can cause medical problems. Doctors have noted that more tranquillizers are given to people living in tower blocks or on modern housing estates than to others. The "new town blues" was a phrase often heard in the 1960s, as people moved into new towns and became bored and fed up with their way of life in new houses. It is a phrase which applies equally well today.

THE GREEN BELT

People do not usually want to live a long way from their job, but sometimes they have no choice. To find a house which they can afford to buy, or even a house at all, means that they have to live in the suburbs or "satellite" towns around the city. Most cities have an area surrounding them which is not developed for housing or industry. This is called the GREEN BELT. It stops urban sprawl, where the city seems to go on endlessly. There are special laws which stop building on the green belt.

PROBLEMS IN TOWNS

Squatters
Young people who look for jobs in towns and cities are not usually interested in a council house or buying their own house, but look for cheap rented accommodation. They want a flat or bedsit not too far from where they work. This is where there is a real shortage. Laws which make things more secure for the tenant (person renting rooms) have caused problems for some landlords. Some prefer not to let their houses or flats at all now that it is difficult to evict the tenants at short notice. There are even fewer flats and bedsits because of this.

Some people have taken the matter into their own hands. Houses which can be lived in, but are left empty, waiting for redevelopment, by the local authority, are taken over by SQUATTERS. Most squatters have nowhere else to go. They would be willing to pay a reasonable rent for decent accommodation if they could find it. Although they sometimes break the law when entering an empty house, once inside they make the place comfortable and fit to live in. They usually pay for water, electricity and gas, and sometimes even pay rates as well. In some areas, councils actually inform the local squatters' groups when houses are empty and unsuitable for their own tenants. This is done on the understanding that the squatters will get out of the property without any fuss when it becomes needed.

Some squatters give the rest a bad name. They go into empty houses and make them even worse, living in filthy and unhygienic conditions. Some councils are not very sympathetic to homeless people either. They smash up the inside of their houses, and make holes in the roof so that the house cannot be lived in. When squatters do move in, these councils get the police or bailiffs to evict them — even if the houses are not to be knocked down for a year or so.

Preservation

Another problem in our towns and cities is whether to preserve older buildings. When space and land are in so much demand, old buildings only 2, 3 or 4 storeys high and with large rooms are not economic. It would perhaps be better to knock them down and build modern office blocks, car parks and flats. This would make a lot of sense, as many of our difficulties in towns are caused by buildings and roads not suited to our modern way of life. On the other hand, it is these very buildings which make our towns what they are. Almost every town in Britain has a variety of buildings put up at different times in our history. They make each town different, and give the towns their character. If they are demolished, then that character goes. This has happened in some of our towns, in some towns in Europe, and in many American towns.

In 1980, Roger Ratcliffe, in the *Sunday Times* wrote:

Almost every amenity society in the central area [of London] is involved in bitter fights with developers to preserve the traditional character of its neighbourhood from the steel girders, poured concrete and reflective glass of the proposed new offices.

Many areas in our towns are threatened with redevelopment. Some old buildings are ugly, have outlived their usefulness, and should possibly be replaced by a well-designed modern building. It is usually cheaper for people to renovate an old building and adapt their plans. But many firms still feel the need for the prestige which they will gain from modern spacious offices in a new tower block.

The Environment

Many are concerned at the way in which young people, especially, react to life in cities and towns. The result of all the planning and careful thought has been a "concrete jungle" to some, which may be lively in the day, but is deserted and desolate at night.

Many young people feel that there is not enough to do in towns. Here they are gathering on a street corner at Toxteth, in Liverpool, just before the riots in July 1981. Look carefully at their surroundings. Is it a pleasant environment?

Young people hang around on street corners looking for something to do, and may end up in trouble with the law. They may live in poor housing and prefer to be out on the streets rather than at home where it is cold and damp. They may be unemployed, and have no money to spend on entertainment. They may be bored, and just out looking for trouble, which could erupt into serious riots as it did in Brixton, Toxteth and Moss-side in 1981. There are no easy solutions for some young people in urban areas. Adventure playgrounds may cater for the younger ones, and youth clubs and discos help others use up their energy.

Making jobs in towns is even more difficult. The old-established industries which used to provide many jobs in towns are now out-of-date. The machinery and way of working are old-fashioned and costly. Many industries have had to close because they were uneconomic, and lots of people lost their jobs. Recently, it has become a little easier to set up a small business in urban areas, and grants and special help are given to those offering work to others. However, it needs many small businesses to offer jobs to the thousands of people who lose theirs in a town when a steelworks shuts down.

Some people think that it is the effect of their ENVIRONMENT which makes the teenagers in places like Toxteth behave as they do. An ugly environment encourages ugly behaviour. Towns and cities may not have been ideal in the past, but now they are too regimented, almost too planned. Large expanses of concrete are broken here and there by flower beds and tubs. There are no large areas of rough ground, bomb sites or derelict buildings where children can play safely and with imagination.

Visual Pollution

People who live in towns often do not see how ugly their surroundings can be. We accept what is familiar to us, and so do not notice things we pass every day on the way to school or work. Ugliness can be a pile of litter blown behind some railings, a row of derelict houses with windows and doors boarded up, slogans sprayed across a wall, telephone wires, street signs and road directions making a confusing mess at a crossroads, or even a badly designed building not fitting in with its surroundings. If people were more aware of the ugliness around them, they might take action to improve their environment.

Other Problems

This chapter has concentrated on only a few of the problems in our towns. Water supply, waste, sewage and refuse disposal, traffic, air, water and noise pollution are also difficulties of living and working in towns. These are dealt with in more detail in the other chapters.

These pictures show better than words some of the visual pollution in our towns and cities.

Transport

ROADS

In the 1970s almost one million people were killed or seriously injured on the roads. Between 1928 and 1980 325,000 people were killed and 12 million injured. As more people own cars, the number of accidents on the roads increases. Twenty-five years ago, a car was a luxury. Nowadays millions of people in Britain own cars, and some families have more than one.

Accidents are not the only problem. The exhaust from cars and lorries badly pollutes the air. Look back at pages 6-7, to check on the ways in which these vehicles POLLUTE.

All these cars need roads. Most of the roads in Britain were built for the horse and cart. Being so much slower than the car, the horse and cart could cope with difficult bends and narrow roads. Today the roads in our villages and towns are often clogged with traffic. They cannot cope with the number of cars, nor the size of the larger lorries. Many towns are now by-passed by dual-carriageways. Motorways have also been built so that people can get from one place to another more quickly. The problem is that by-passes and motorways use a great deal of land — often valuable agricultural land. About 10 hectares (25 acres) are used for every mile of motorway, and that does not include the land used for junctions and service stations.

Motorways and a better road network have made places more accessible. In the past, most goods were moved by rail, but the trend has been for goods to be moved by road, by larger and larger lorries. These cause congestion, pollute the air, and break up the road surface. Some people now think that most goods should again be carried by rail; and that the government should give a subsidy to encourage this. People whose homes are shaken by heavy lorries — JUGGERNAUTS — every minute of the day and night, feel especially strongly about this. The people who use lorries, and the firms that provide transport believe that it is easier and quicker to carry goods by lorry from one factory to another or from a warehouse to a shop. It is possible that the railway will be used more, as oil — and so derv for the lorries — becomes more expensive.

Problems often arise when a new road is proposed. Those people who have been disturbed by the noise, smell, and vibration of heavy traffic on the road it is to replace are relieved to think that they may live quietly at last. Others are worried that their homes may be knocked down to make way for the new road, or that some or all of their land may be taken. Even worse is to find, when the new road is built, that you are living within a few

The village of Bridge is on the A2, near Canterbury, and so on the main route to Europe. Lorries like this one thunder through the narrow streets — but by-passes cost a lot of money.

Motorways use up a great deal of land, and service stations even more. This is the Strensham Service Station on the M5.

Many people had to put up with noise and inconvenience when Westway was built. It cut through existing houses and communities, as you can see in this photograph. When it was finished, it was easier for traffic to get in and out of London from the west, but some people had to be rehoused. They hung banners from their upstairs windows which could be seen on the Westway. The banners read "Get us out of this hell". Their homes were so close to the road that the traffic disrupted their normal way of life.

metres of juggernauts thundering past the window. This is what happened, for example, when the Western Avenue Extension (Westway) was opened in London in 1970.

With car ownership, our pattern of life has changed. People used to be able to buy their everyday needs — bread, meat, vegetables — from a row of shops, which could be reached on foot. They may have travelled to the larger town or city centre at the weekend to do more important shopping — to buy clothes and furniture, for example. Now, as more people travel by car, the town or city centre has changed. In many places there are large multi-storey car parks around a shopping area, which may be for pedestrians only. Shops in these centres provide almost all the goods people want to buy. The shops arrange a

"carry out" service, allow customers to wheel all their shopping back to their cars in trolleys, or arrange special "pick-up points". Having made the effort, most people do not then feel like shopping every day of the week. The food they buy each week, or even each month, is stored at home in fridges and freezers. Small local shops and shopping centres which cannot be reached easily by car lose out to more accessible shops. Sometimes even these more accessible shops are forced to close because people prefer to shop in specially built shopping centres. Here shops which seem like warehouses supply people's shopping needs — from groceries to clothes and furniture. These are usually built out of town and can only be reached by car, or specially arranged buses. Because they take up so much land, there are few of these hypermarkets in the southeast.

RAILWAYS

In 1900 there were 1,115 million rail passenger journeys.

In 1920 there were 2,186 million rail passenger journeys.

In 1975 there were 715 million rail passenger journeys.

Most of the railways in Britain were built between 1830 and 1900. There were a number of rail companies and they often dupli-

Freightliners are loaded at the factory, and taken by rail to many parts of the country. They can be loaded also directly onto ships — saving time and money.

cated lines. A complicated network of railways resulted. The idea was that each town should have a railway station, and every village should be within a day's journey of a station by horse and cart.

Railway lines and stations are expensive to maintain. In 1963 Dr Beeching published a special report on the railways. He suggested keeping open only those railway lines between the large towns, and closing stations and routes which did not make a profit. The argument which the *Beeching Plan* provoked is one which still continues today. Should the railways be run like a business to make money; or should they provide a social service?

Running a commuter service is not always profitable. Many trains have to run in the few hours in the morning and evening when people travel to and from work. Yet the stations have to be manned and the track maintained all through the daytime too, when fewer people travel by train. The enormous stations in London are jammed with commuters in the morning and evening, yet are much quieter during the day. Recent large increases in rail fares in the south-east reflect this uneconomic use of the railway. It is difficult to get people to work in central London. Transport costs are high, and the journey can take a long time. Some people feel that tax allowances should be made for season ticket travel to London. Others think that there should be a government subsidy to make the rail fares cheaper.

Railway lines between large towns and cities usually make more money than commuter lines. British Rail have developed the Inter-city service especially for business people. The trains are new, comfortable, and well-designed, with tables between facing seats. Work can be done in comfort during the journey. Many people prefer to travel by train than fly. Airports are some way out of the main town centre, and so travelling there takes time. Parking may be a problem at an airport, and "checking in" can take minutes as well. By contrast, arriving by taxi at a main

city station and walking straight on to a train takes very little time — as long as the train is there!

British Rail have also developed goods and parcel transport. It is cheaper to move bulk goods by rail, than it is by lorry. If a factory is on a railway line, it can take advantage of the FREIGHTLINER service. The customer loads the goods at the factory into a CONTAINER. These have to be a special size — 2.4 metres high, 2.4 metres wide and 3,6,9 or 12 metres long — so that they fit into the railway wagons. When they are ready, the containers are lifted by crane onto flat-bed wagons. The same process in reverse takes place at the other end of the journey. The containers can also be loaded directly onto ships from the railway, which saves time and money. Freightliners run to a regular timetable, usually at night.

Every passenger train carries letters and parcels in the guard's van, but some trains carry only parcels. Parcels from London are brought to the main terminal stations where they are sorted and coded to show which station the parcel is going to. Once the parcels are loaded on the trains, delivery can be very quick, often overnight.

WATER TRANSPORT

Many of the people who built the first railways in the 1800s had also been digging the canals. The "navvies" had "navigated" the canals through the country. They built bridges, aqueducts, and excavated tunnels. The narrow boat which was used to transport goods on the canals was only 2.1 metres wide. Usually the narrow boat man would take his wife and children with him on the boat. The living quarters were clearly very cramped.

Moving goods around the country by canal was cheap. A horse on the canal bank would pull the narrow boat, and the boats travelled surprisingly quickly, because the routes were so direct.

In European countries canals are still an

important means of transport. The canals and boats are wide, and a lot of bulky goods like coal and gravel are moved by barge. It is very economical to use barges, and the average journey is as long as 321 kilometres. In Britain today only short lengths of the original canal network are used. The journeys themselves are shorter, an average of only 16 kilometres. It would be very expensive to widen the canals and the locks to take bigger boats. Some canals are still used for pleasure — for fishing and narrow boat holidays, for example. Many of the canals and locks, though, are unusable. Environmental groups have been clearing locks and canals to try to get canals used again. This may be possible if the road and rail systems in Britain become inadequate.

Some river transport is still important in Britain, but this is mainly on a local level. However, sea transport is still the most important way in which goods are carried between Britain and the rest of the world. Ships have become so much bigger that many of the older and traditional ports are now too small to handle them. The docks in London, for example the Surrey Docks and Royal Docks, are now closed and lying idle. Docks further downstream, near the mouth of the River Thames at Tilbury, are used instead.

Goods such as oil and grain are loaded onto ships in bulk, directly by pipe-line. Others are put into CONTAINERS, taken to the dock by train and loaded by crane. All this has speeded up the shiploading process.

AIR TRANSPORT

Heathrow is the world's biggest international airport; some 27 million people passed through it in 1979. The airport has grown to its present size in a remarkably short time. Some people who worked at Heathrow when it opened in 1946 remember the airport then. Mushrooms grew between the runways, there was a cabbage patch at the end of Runway One, and tents were put up as the terminals. Now, Terminal Three alone has 93,000 square

On the Aire and Calder canal, linking Leeds to Goole, commercial barges deliver coal to the power station at Ferrybridge.

metres of public space. Two runways are used — one for taking off and the other for landing. At peak periods aeroplanes take off every minute.

Perhaps the biggest change in passenger transport has been with air travel. Countries which were days and weeks away by ship and train, can now be reached in a matter of hours. Some businessmen commute between London and cities such as New York, San Francisco, Hong Kong and Singapore. Places in the Mediterranean have become popular holiday resorts because of cheap air travel. Package tours are the same price, or only a little more than the scheduled air fare.

Aeroplanes are still quite small to carry bulky cargo, and only 10% of the UK's overseas trade is carried by air. As the planes become bigger, more cargo may be carried.

The increase in air travel has meant problems for those living around airports. Airports provide jobs — over 56,000 are employed just to run Heathrow — and these people must live reasonably close to their work. But people coming and going to Heathrow cause congestion in the surrounding roads, and the planes cause noise pollution. (See pages 14-15.) Concorde is an aeroplane which flies at twice the speed of sound, or SUPERSONICALLY.

Passengers in Concorde reach other countries more quickly than they would in ordinary subsonic aeroplanes. On the other hand, by moving so quickly, Concorde creates SOUND WAVES which disturb people on its flight path. Some people feel very strongly that Concorde should never have been built because it was so expensive and because of the pollution. The business people who travel in Concorde appreciate its luxury and the extra time they have because of the shorter journey.

HOVERCRAFT

The hovercraft is an important British invention. It can travel both on land and sea at high speeds, certainly quicker than a normal boat. Unfortunately, it is not used as much as its inventor hoped it would be. Its main use in Britain is on the Cross-Channel Ferry to France, where the journey takes only 35-40 minutes compared with the ferryboat time of two or more hours. Wide-bodied hovercraft are now used which can take larger vehicles and many passengers.

The number 1 departure lounge at Heathrow is crowded with people waiting for aeroplanes to take them to Europe.

Natural Resources

There are three types of natural resources which support us:

(i) The living things, including ourselves, which inhabit the earth.
(ii) All the materials which make up the earth's crust and the atmosphere.
(iii) The energy to do work and supply power.

These resources are not evenly distributed over the earth's surface, so that all countries do not have an equal share. They are also not all renewable; that means that they run out. When William of Normandy fought Harold of England at the Battle of Hastings in 1066, much of England was covered with woods and forests. Hunting in these forests was a favourite sport of Kings and Queens. When Henry VIII wanted to develop England's navy, there was plenty of English oak to cut down for the ships. Today, there are few areas of natural woodland, and even those woods remaining often have to be protected as special conservation areas. The Forestry Commission have planted large areas of land with trees, to try to supply Britain with the wood that is needed — but we still have to import a large amount from other countries. In any event, the planted trees take many years to grow before they can be used.

Wood can be supplied by planting new trees. Other resources are not renewable at all. Many of the metals used in industry are gradually being used up, and there is concern about what will happen when they run out completely. The more we use these resources, the quicker they will run out. By limiting the population and so the overall demand, we can make our NATURAL RESOURCES last longer.

LIVING THINGS

We rely on many other living things for our life. We eat plants and animals, have animals as pets, and grow plants in our leisure. Living things add much to our quality of life as well as giving us food. There is more information on the way in which plants and animals provide us with food on pages 32-35. But the plants and animals do not exist merely to vary our diet, or to be used by us. It is because some people think this that there are a great number of ENDANGERED SPECIES.

You sometimes hear the expression "Dead as a Dodo". The dodo was a strange-looking bird which lived on the island of Mauritius. It did not have wings, and so was easy for people to hunt and kill. The last dodo was seen in 1681. Other animals have been killed so that they are now EXTINCT. The Red Data Book is produced by the World Wildlife

Fund. It lists all the endangered species, like the tiger, the orangutan, the polar bear, the snow leopard. These animals are in danger because people have killed many of them or destroyed the areas where they live. We kill these animals for fashion, clothes, jewellery, or for the chemicals they give which we can use. Wild animals are not often killed for food. If they take our food, we kill them. Their ENVIRONMENT is changed when reservoirs are built for water supply and power, when forests and scrubland are cleared for farming, when roads are built to get to valuable mineral ores and when those ores are mined. It is up to us to make sure that the world's wildlife is protected.

The ways in which the animals are killed are not always pleasant. In Africa, elephants are killed by poachers, who hack out the tusks, and leave the elephant to rot. Some-

times they do not even make sure that the elephant is dead. Wardens in the Safari Parks in Africa say that it is sickening to see an elephant like this. The poachers kill any elephant for the ivory. They may take a mother still nursing her baby. Then the baby elephant may die too, because it cannot support or defend itself on its own.

Wild animals are killed for the value of their fur. A coat made out of leopard, ocelot or jaguar will cost tens of thousands of pounds. In the 1960s 15,000 ocelot skins were exported each year from just one port in Peru, South America. When the price for each kind of skin rose, farmers left their farms, bought piano wire and set up choke snares in the bush to make money instead from the animal skins. There are more details about the problems caused by hunting whales on page 27. Other sea creatures, like the dolphin, are dealt with in a similar way. In 1980, there were protests to Japan from all over the world. The fishermen in Japan had killed over

About 100 dolphins were killed at Iki island in Japan. Here a fisherman stabs a dolphin. The dolphins eat yellowtail fish and squid, which the men catch too.

1,000 dolphins. They said that the dolphins ate the fish that they wanted to catch. They were a pest and were killed in the same way that rats, mice and foxes might be killed.

SUPERSONIC (sound) waves of 24 kilohertz have kept the dolphins away from the fishing areas in the past and have not harmed them. The Japanese caught some of the dolphins and kept them in a net in the sea. They tested the dolphins with supersonic waves of 75, 115 and even 200 kilohertz. The sound waves caused the dolphins to "dash themselves helplessly into the nets enclosing their small area of confinement, with no way of escaping the terrifying sounds".

Limiting the number of people in the world would make the demand for natural resources increase at a slower rate. At the moment, the world population is increasing very fast. There are almost 4,000 million in the world today, and every year, the population grows by about 2%. The world already has problems which are made worse by too many people.

At least half the people in the world do not have enough to eat. It is possible that the time will come when there are too many people for the earth to support.

In Britain the population is growing very, very slowly. Yet we still have serious problems with housing and unemployment. Much of our food has to be bought in from other countries, even though British farmers are very efficient. Many people are concerned at the world distribution of food and other resources.

In February 1980, Prince Philip, as President of the British Appeal of the World Wildlife Fund, launched the "World Conservation Strategy". More than 1,000 animal SPECIES, and at least 25,000 plant species are threatened with extinction. At least 25 of the world's

Coal has been mined for centuries as a source of power. Here the old coal mine at Cwm Colliery, West Glamorgan, contrasts with the beautiful scenery in the background.

major fishing areas have been OVER-FISHED. The annual catch is 20% down on what it might be. Deserts are spreading, threatening the lives of 600 million people who live on the edges of deserts. The "World Conservation Strategy" proposes to look at existing conservation laws, bring in stronger international laws, and plan and measure the use of NATURAL RESOURCES.

MATERIALS

The materials in the earth's crust include all the minerals and fuel supplies which we use. As we become more advanced in technology, use more machines, and have a higher standard of living, we use more and more materials.

Oil, gas and coal occur naturally in the rocks of the earth's surface. They were formed in similar ways. Tiny sea creatures died and sank to the bottom of the sea millions of years ago. Gradually, they became covered with layers of sand and mud. The weight of these layers, and the movements of the earth's crust changed the sand and mud into rock, and the dead creatures into gas and tiny drops of oil. Coal comes from trees. Trees decayed, died, and fell into swamps millions of years ago. The water in the swamp stopped the trees rotting away completely. Mud and silt built up in the swamp, and it too was covered by sand. All these layers became rock, and the trees changed to coal.

Coal, gas and oil are NON-RENEWABLE RESOURCES. This means that, as it takes millions of years for coal, gas and oil to form, there will be no more supplies when present ones have been used up. Metals and mineral ores are also non-renewable. It has been estimated that some of these minerals will not be easily available within the next twenty years. People are already using low-grade ores — that is, rock containing only a small proportion of the mineral. The highest-grade deposits of copper, zinc, lead, tin, molybdenum and mercury are already almost all used. Copper ores with 1.5% copper were mined in the 1920s. Now the ore contains only 0.75%.

These are estimates of how long the reserves of important resources will last, if used at the present rate:

Lead	until the year		1990
Uranium	"	"	" 1990
Silver	"	"	" 1990
Gold	"	"	" 1990
Tin	"	"	" 2000
Copper	"	"	" 2000
Natural Gas	"	"	" 2000
Oil	"	"	" 2000
Zinc	"	"	" 2000

Oil, natural gas and coal are fuels which can be burnt to give us power. Oil and coal can be made into other things as well: medicines, pesticides, detergents, paints, man-made fibres and plastic. Oil is also used as fuel for cars, lorries, trains and aeroplanes.

Important industries need metals. Chromium is used in the manufacture of stainless steel. Columbium, another metal, is used in turbine blades. Most of the metal fittings in cars are made from zinc. Lead is used as an effective shield against radiation, as well as in batteries. Tin has a variety of uses, apart from the tin-plated can. Manganese is essential to the manufacture of steel. The US Geological Survey said: "The element [manganese] is essential to the whole industrial capacity of the world . . . when we can do without steel, we can do without manganese." Copper is used in the engineering and electrical industries. A television set, for example, contains about half a kilogram of copper.

Less metal is needed as components in machines, such as resistors and capacitors, become smaller. Some metals can be replaced by plastic. Sometimes plastic does the job better than the original metal. But it would be wrong to think that it does not matter using up all these metals because they can be replaced by a man-made product. RE-CYCLING is one answer to the shortage of minerals. But it is expensive to separate out our rubbish. This is considered in more detail on page 64.

To build a special machine that separates glass, rags, paper, metals and plastic costs millions of pounds. Such machines do pay for themselves eventually, but many local authorities cannot afford this amount of money. As the cost of raw materials increases, and metals get more and more difficult to find, it may become worthwhile to save these precious metals from our WASTE.

ENERGY

The energy to supply power usually comes as electricity, although coal, oil, gas and wood also provide energy. As the standard of living improves, the demand for electricity goes up. In the 1950s most people had electric light in their homes, possibly an electric cooker, fridge, television and radio, but not much else. Now, many people have stereo equipment, hairdryers, washing machines, kettles and toasters. Some may have dishwashers, tumble dryers, food mixers. Others even have electric tin openers, knife sharpeners, carving knives and toothbrushes. All of these appliances use electricity. Industry, too, is using more electricity, as it becomes more automated.

Power stations produce electricity by burning FOSSIL FUEL, like coal, oil or natural gas. The heat produced turns water into steam. This steam spins a turbine which turns a generator, and so electricity is made. When the steam cools back to water, it can be used again. Oil and natural gas resources are being worked out. Coal will last for much longer, but already people are looking for new supplies of energy.

Energy from the sea is considered on page 28.

The sun is the greatest source of energy — SOLAR ENERGY. Green plants have used this energy for millions of years, but they only use 1% of the sun's energy; the rest is lost. People are becoming more interested in solar energy. Solar panels to collect solar energy can now be fitted into ordinary

The Laboratory of Solar Energy at Odeillo Font-Romeu in France produces electricity from the sun.

The machinery of the hydro-electric power station is situated inside the mountain at Ben Cruachan. A tunnel links the power station with the outside, and a large part of the mountain was removed so that the power station could be housed.

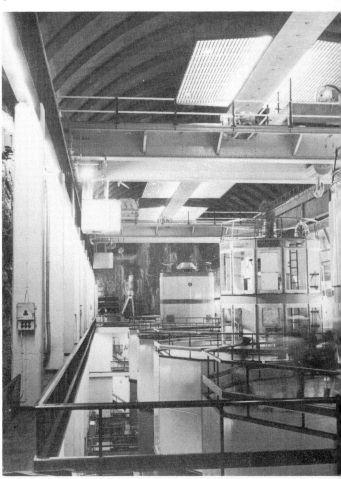

houses. The panels are fixed onto the roof, and use the warmth from the sun to heat water and the central heating system. On a larger scale, solar furnaces use reflecting mirrors. These focus the sun's rays onto a small area which heats the water to drive turbines and so produce electricity. There is a solar furnace like this in the Pyrenees, in France.

HYDRO-ELECTRIC POWER uses falling water to drive the turbines. Usually a dam is built so that the water supply is constant. The water falls down pipes from the RESERVOIR of water behind the dam. At the bottom of the pipes is the electricity-generating machinery. At Ben Cruachan in Scotland, the water is pumped back up into the storage reservoir at night. The demand for electricity falls when most people are asleep, and so pumping the water back up uses surplus electricity.

Wind, too, is a source of energy. In many areas, for centuries, the power from windmills was the main way to grind corn or pump water. Although it is unlikely that windmills will compete with power stations, they do provide a cheap energy source. Sites for windmills have to be chosen carefully, and many people do not want to live close to a windmill where it will be very windy. Those who want to see wind power used by more people are trying to produce a more refined windmill.

Another source of energy is NUCLEAR ENERGY. The smallest particle of any element of matter is the atom. In the atom, a nucleus of neutrons and protons is surrounded by electrons. The neutrons and protons are kept together by nuclear binding forces. Nuclear energy is released when a heavy atom breaks into two (fission) or when two light atoms join together (fusion). It is difficult for the neutrons and protons to hold together in a heavy atom. They tend to be naturally unstable or RADIOACTIVE. This means that they give out RADIATION, and change into slightly different atoms. The rate at which a radioactive atom changes or decays may be very low — sometimes it takes mil-

lions of years. If the atom is hit by a neutron, though, it will break into two parts instantly. The neutrons from fission hit other atoms and so the process goes on. This chain action creates a great deal of heat, and this heat turns water into steam, which eventually makes electricity. Exactly the same process is used in a nuclear power station as in a nuclear bomb. However, the power station controls the explosion.

In Britain there are 14 different nuclear power stations. Some are Magnox Reactors and some Advanced Gas-cooled Reactors (AGRs). The Magnox reactors use natural uranium metal, in rods, which are put into cases of MAGNesium OXide. AGRs use specially processed, or enriched, uranium. By the end of 1981, nuclear power produced about 15% of the total electricity in England and Wales.

Although Britain has had nuclear power stations for a number of years, people are still worried about the problems of using radioactive fuel. Not all radiation is dangerous, but some can cause cancer and mutations and, eventually, or in large doses, death. Mutations are changes in the genetic code. All living things have a genetic code. It makes sure that children are like their parents — humans as well as animals and plants. An atomic bomb was exploded on the Bikini Islands, in the Pacific Ocean, in 1954. When scientists returned to the islands much later, they found that a lot of the wildlife had returned. But the wildlife was not normal; there had been mutations. Most of the birds were sterile, and so, although they laid eggs, these did not hatch. Some of the hatched eggs contained deformed birds, which soon died. Turtles usually return to the sea after laying their eggs on land. On the islands, turtles were dead and dying far inland. They had been affected by radiation when they were born and had not formed a normal behaviour pattern.

In dealing with any radioactive material there is the danger of coming into contact with radiation. The nuclear power industry is very safety-conscious. The fuel is transported in special containers. People who work in the power station wear protective clothing, are protected by thick lead screens, and have regular medical checks. There is always the danger of a mistake or an accident. Nuclear power stations in Britain have had accidental leaks of radioactive material. These have contaminated the people who work in the station and the surrounding countryside. Sometimes the power station has to be closed, so that the source of the leak can be found.

In Harrisburg, in America, in 1979, the worst possible accident almost happened. One of the cooling pipes cracked, and the temperature of the radioactive fuel rose. The fuel itself began to melt, and hot radioactive gases formed. People from a large area were evacuated, and police patrolled the streets to stop any looting. For almost a week there was the danger of a melt-down in which tons of white-hot radioactive material would burn their way into the earth. The melt-down is called the "CHINA SYNDROME", because jokingly, some people think that it could burn through to China. Fortunately, the process was stopped and the material cooled — but the worst almost did happen.

Another problem is how to get rid of the radioactive WASTE. The waste can be radioactive gases, solids or liquids. Gases are discharged high into the atmosphere. Liquids and solids are stored under supervision, buried, or dumped at sea. The problem is that they can be radioactive almost indefinitely. In May 1978 Parliament decided to allow British Nuclear Fuels Limited to process waste nuclear fuel at Windscale in Cumbria. Radioactive waste fuel from other countries is sent to Windscale, where it is separated into re-usable fuel and waste. The re-usable fuel is then sent back to the power stations. This process will reduce the amount of very active radioactive waste which has to be stored, buried or dumped. It does, however, mean that Britain will be bringing in very dangerous waste from other countries.

Another problem with radioactive fuel is that it may be used to make a nuclear bomb. Various amounts of fuel have been "lost", even though very strict precautions are taken. At first, scientists did not think that nuclear fuel could be used to make bombs, but in May 1974 India exploded a test bomb which had been made with nuclear fuel. A lot of people are worried that nuclear waste moving around the world could fall into the "wrong" hands and be used by terrorists.

Despite all these problems, nuclear power does produce electricity reasonably efficiently, and our resources of oil and gas will not last much longer. Some people think that the problems far outweigh this advantage.

Many people are worried about nuclear power and the effects it may have on the environment. Here people are protesting about nuclear waste from other countries being processed at Windscale. Often people feel that the only way they can get attention for their views is by marching and protesting in this way.

Waste

On the morning of Friday, 21 October 1966, at 9.15, 28 adults and 116 children were killed. They were buried under the waste from the coal mine nearby. It had rained a lot, and the water had seeped into the coal tip. The wet sludge moved downhill, slowly at first, and then quicker. It covered the school at Aberfan, in South Wales, and some of the houses on the same road.

Aberfan, 1966. Eight terraced houses are buried beneath the slag on the left of this picture. Heavy rain water made the waste from a nearby coal mine move downhill. A primary school was covered by the slag, and a corner of the secondary school, on the right of the picture, was hit as well.

This was a shocking effect of the results of our WASTE. People have always produced waste. Only when the population grew and industry developed did waste become a problem. We are now using our resources more quickly than ever before, and as well as looking for new sources we need to RECYCLE our waste. As more people produce more waste, the natural processes which break down the waste cannot cope, and this waste must be dealt with efficiently and effectively.

SEWAGE

When people live in small villages, getting rid of their personal waste — sewage — is not a big problem. In towns there are more people, and so more sewage. If sewage is not treated properly, it can contaminate water and cause disease and death. Typhoid and cholera are both diseases which can be found in impure water. The symptoms of cholera are dizziness with sudden diarrhoea. This is followed by muscle cramps and possible death in a few hours. Typhoid develops more slowly. A headache, constipation, perhaps a nosebleed, are followed by a rise in temperature. After a few days' diarrhoea, stomach pains and a rash may occur. Neither cholera nor typhoid are found in Britain's water supply today, but in 1831 50,000 people died from these diseases in London alone. A doctor, John Snow, had been studying cholera, and thought that it could be carried in water. He studied the cholera epidemic in London in 1854. Over 500 people in a small area of Soho had died in 10 days. Most of the people who had died had got their drinking water from one pump. Dr Snow suggested removing the handle from the pump so that the water could not be used, and the number of deaths fell rapidly.

Sewage was first dealt with on SEWAGE FARMS. The sewage was taken out of the town by pipes to a sewage farm. On the sewage farm the sewage trickled over the ground. By the time the water from the sewage reached a river or water in the rocks underground, it was hoped that all the impurities had gone.

As towns grew bigger, and there was even more sewage, the sewage farms could not cope. Proper SEWAGE TREATMENT WORKS were built. These used less land than the sewage farms and could treat more sewage.

There are laws which stop local authorities putting large amounts of untreated sewage into rivers. Most towns have some sort of sewage treatment works. Towns on the coast, however, sometimes dump sewage straight into the sea. When the pipe carrying the sewage — the OUTFALL PIPE — goes a long way into the sea, the action of the sea water treats the sewage. At some seaside resorts, the outfall pipe is not long enough, and there have been cases of people swimming in the sea close to untreated sewage.

The Crossness Sewage Treatment Works is on the south bank of the River Thames. It was first opened in 1865, and the new biological treatment works was opened in 1964. Most of the sewage from south London flows to Crossness in three huge pipes, 3.5 metres in diameter. Each day 522,000,000 litres are treated. This is over 318 litres per person (in the area served by Crossness) per day.

This diagram shows how crude sewage is processed through the Crossness Sewage Treatment Works. The liquid is pumped into the River Thames, and the treated solids, now sludge, is dumped in the North Sea.

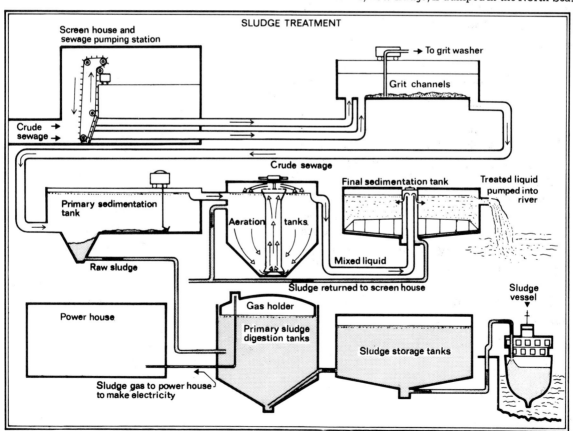

First of all, stones, rags and other large items which have been thrown down drains (such as tyres, broken bicycles, large stones) are removed by screens. The screens are closely spaced bars. The sewage flows on to the grit channels. Here, the channel's shape, and the rate of flow of the sewage, result in the deposit of grit and sand washed off the roads. This grit is washed and used for land reclamation. In the Primary Sedimentation Tanks, the solids in the sewage settle. Liquid and solids are then treated differently. The liquid goes on to the Aeration Tanks. The liquid is mixed with special bacteria for 7 hours, and air is forced into this mixture. The organic matter settles out in the Final Sedimentation Tanks. The liquid is pumped into the River Thames, and the organic matter is piped to the sludge from the Primary Sedimentation Tanks. This sludge goes to the Sludge Digestion Tanks. At a temperature of 32°C, the sludge ferments for 16 days. Methane gas is produced — which provides power for the sewage treatment process. The sludge itself, now harmless, is pumped onto boats (called "Bovril boats") and dumped out at sea.

RUBBISH

Dealing with litter and the rubbish people dump is expensive. It now costs about £100 million a year to collect and dispose of this rubbish. People cannot avoid producing sewage, but they can put their other rubbish in the proper place. The local authorities arrange to collect large items from houses; sometimes they charge a small fee. Even still, some people dump their unwanted rubbish in the country.

This is a list of the rubbish which was removed from a half-mile stretch of a stream in a city:

8 bed springs	3 gas fires
9 mattresses	7 washing machines
18 cushions	5 fridges
4 feather pillows	4 vacuum cleaners
3 easychairs	15 cookers
1 couch	3 televisions
9 wooden chairs & stools	7 prams
6 electric fires	hundreds of plastic containers
hundreds of bottles	5 tricycles
4 bags of cement	breeze blocks
8 sinks	concrete slabs
5 toilet pans	1 garden roller
14 stone fireplaces	tons of garden refuse
plastic pipes	shopping bags
stone pipes	wire baskets
20 carpets	1 complete car in pieces
1 car engine	62 tyres
9 car bonnets & doors	46 1-gallon oil drums
50 oil filters	bricks
pots and pans	doors
garden fences	trees
railway sleepers	tar
wood	clothes
8 corrugated sheets	bits of metal
papers	
cardboard boxes	

It cost a lot of money to clear this.

A few years ago the "Keep Britain Tidy" group ran a campaign with the slogan "My little wrapper won't do any harm". It is when a lot of people drop little wrappers that litter becomes a problem. Litter is not only unsightly; it is also dangerous. An empty paper bag can blow across a windscreen on a windy day and cause a car accident. People are cut by broken glass and metal cans at the seaside or in a park. Animals, too, can be hurt. Farm animals have been suffocated by plastic bags. Birds have got their beaks caught in the ring-pull of a can. Small wild animals go inside empty drink bottles, looking for food, and then become trapped.

Most of the food we buy today is in some form of ▶ packaging. Often this is for hygienic reasons, or for ease of handling, but it is not always necessary.

62

PACKAGING

Much of our waste comes from the packaging around the things we buy. During the war, when paper, plastic and metal were scarce, shops sold most of their goods loose. Any paper bags that were used were saved carefully to be used again. Now, most of the things sold in shops are packaged — partly to encourage people to buy them. Fruit is put on a polystyrene tray and covered with clear plastic film. Eyeshadow is placed in a small metal container, onto a plastic tray, into a plastic case, then into a box, and finally may be covered with clear plastic. Sometimes the goods that are sold are put in packaging for good reasons. Delicate stereo equipment is packaged in expanded polystyrene to protect it. Bread in supermarkets is hygienically wrapped in plastic bags. Packaging cuts down on damage and losses to the goods during transport. It is essential in self-service shops — reducing time and labour. It contains the goods and identifies them. On the other hand, oranges and lemons have their own packaging — their skin.

The Editor of *Packaging News*, a trade journal, said: "Packaging extends the benefits of mass marketing. Without packaging self-service would be impossible, there would be far fewer foods and other commodities to choose from, and the cost of distributing the myriad products we now take for granted would go up even more rapidly than the cost of the products themselves."

The following figures show what percentage of the total cost of goods in the shops is spent on packaging:

Beer in a tinplate can	43%
Beer in a non-return glass bottle	36%
Baby food in a glass jar	36%
Motor oil in a metal can	26%
Paint in an aerosol can	16%
Breakfast cereal in folding carton	15%
Toy in film-wrapped carton	14%

Paper and board are the materials most used for packaging. Plastic is replacing glass and metals. A plastic bottle is one tenth the weight of a glass bottle, and uses less energy being manufactured. When the plastic used is PVC, one of the by-products is mercury, which can pollute rivers and the sea. Glass bottles can be washed, sterilized and used again. Most glass bottles, though, are designed to be thrown away. No-deposit bottles mean no collection, transport, or washing and sterilizing costs for the manufacturer. A returnable soft-drinks bottle makes 50 round trips. The average milk bottle makes 14 trips to customers, and so its cost is spread over 14 pints of milk.

Bottles, cans, paper, plastic bags, plastic cups, aerosol cans are nearly always thrown away. This looks unsightly, and dealing with such litter is expensive. The materials used to make bottles, cans, paper, and so on come from NATURAL RESOURCES, so it is wasteful not to re-use them.

About 6,500 million glass bottles are made every year. 75% of them are non-returnable. Glass is made from sand and limestone which is dug out of the ground. This is often unsightly, as well as sometimes being a waste of good farming land.

7,500 million cans are made every year — and these all end up in the dustbin. 90% of the goods we buy in cans in Britain are sold in returnable glass containers in Norway.

Plastics have a number of advantages — insulation, fire resistance, ability to withstand acids, and durability. This last advantage is the problem. Most plastics are not BIODEGRADABLE. This means that they do not rot naturally. 2,000 plastic cups per person, per year, are thrown away. Recently, a special plastic has been developed which decomposes in sunlight. Most plastics are made from oil; when oil runs out, plastics can then be made from coal, wood and even refuse.

RECYCLING

It takes 17 trees to produce one tonne of paper — enough to make 7,000 copies of a national newspaper. More trees are needed to make paper and board than are being planted. Yet 60% of Britain's domestic refuse is paper and board which is buried.

Only 28% of the paper which we use is collected and used again — RE-CYCLED. Some local authorities collect waste for re-cycling. In the London Borough of Greenwich, glass bottles can be left in large skips — "Bottle Banks" — to be re-cycled. Tin cans can be re-cycled. They can be extracted by magnets from domestic refuse, and the steel and tin recovered by detinning.

DEALING WITH RUBBISH

Most of our rubbish is not re-cycled. It is put in dustbins and collected by the local authority. 90% of rubbish is dumped onto land. Sometimes it is used to fill up holes, which may be dis-used gravel or chalk quarries.

Sometimes rubbish is used to reclaim land from the sea, or to make part of a sea wall. The Ministry of Health, some years ago, recommended a special way of tipping rubbish. High fences made of chicken wire should surround the tip, to collect any rubbish blown by the wind. Each day the rubbish tipped on to land should be squashed flat by bulldozers. Soil should then be used to cover the rubbish.

Some local authorities pulverize their rubbish. The waste is broken up or shredded by a machine, and then dumped. It is easier to flatten pulverized rubbish, and it does not use so much land.

A few authorities burn, or incinerate, their rubbish in special incinerators. Metals can then be separated from the ashes by magnets. In Nottingham the heat from such an incinerator heats a nearby housing estate.

Only a few local authorities compost the rubbish they collect. Screens remove the bulky items, and others — like cans, plastic, glass — have to be removed by hand. Air and water, or sewage sludge are added to the waste, which is put in a large rotating drum. After 5 days, the waste can be used as a soil conditioner.

Waste glass can be re-cycled using bottle banks like this one. In 1979 this bottle bank was "opened" by the Mayor of Brent. Each year over 610 million bottles and jars, or 175,000 tonnes of glass, could be re-cycled in the Greater London Council area.

Household rubbish is unloaded at the Newport Rubbish Tip in Gwent.

Even so, the problem of dealing with our rubbish is not at an end. When there are problems about emptying dustbins, the waste builds up in the streets. This is unsightly and unhygienic. Rats, flies and birds — all carriers of disease — are attracted to the rubbish.

Some tips cause problems in themselves. There have been accidents at the large tip in Essex which deals with industrial TOXIC (poisonous) waste. One lorry driver died in his cab when he dumped a mixture of aluminium oxide and sulphuric acid. This was not dangerous in itself, but was dumped on top of a previous load that contained sulphides. The result was the poisonous gas, hydrogen sulphide.

Factories and waste disposal firms do not always bother to take their dangerous loads to these special tips. FLY-TIPPING occurs when lorry drivers dump their toxic loads in streams, at the side of roads, and in ordinary council tips. Large drums of the poison cyanide, which were leaking, were dumped on waste land next to a children's playground.

CLEANING UP THE CAPITAL

Litter is an EYESORE. It is unpleasant to walk along a street where there is a lot of mess. In some places in London the pavement is so full of boxes and plastic sacks of rubbish that people have to walk in the road.

Westminster Council already spends £5 million a year collecting 160,000 tonnes of rubbish. Problems are caused when cars park on double yellow lines so that the dustcarts cannot get through to pick up the rubbish. Some shops and restaurants use the pavement as their rubbish store, and put out their waste too early in the day. Before it can be cleared away, the rubbish is kicked all over the road, and sometimes it is set on fire.

In May 1980 the Secretary for the Environment started a "Cleaner London" campaign. Volunteers started by cleaning the streets around Piccadilly Circus. There was a Bottle Bank in Leicester Square, and a special anti-litter film was shown in cinemas.

People were able to sponsor litter bins. A lamp-post bin with the sponsor's name on it cost £25, a free-standing pavement bin £50, and a very snazzy double bin £200.

Sponsoring litter bins has two main purposes — there are more litter bins for people to use, and they provide advertising space for a local firm or industry. In addition to this, people become aware of litter, and so may use the bin.

Glossary

Anaerobic without oxygen or air. An anaerobic process is a process which is carried out without any air or oxygen.

Asbestosis a disease which occurs after breathing in the tiny fibres of asbestos. Blue asbestos is particularly harmful, and it has been virtually banned in the UK.

Biodegradable describes something which breaks down or rots naturally. Examples are leaves, wood, paper, vegetables.

"China Syndrome" The worst accident in a nuclear power station will be when the reactor core overheats. The white-hot radioactive material will melt and burn down into the earth. The melt-down is called the "China Syndrome" as a "joke", because China is on the other side of the world from America. Perhaps the Chinese call it the "America Syndrome".

Clean air air which is not polluted. Crusty lichens grow where the air is cleanest, and so they are used as an indicator for clean air.

Conserve, Conservation keeping or protecting areas of land, buildings, animals, plants and so on from harm and/or change.

Constant noise an unwanted sound which goes on all the time. For example, the noise of traffic on a busy road, an electric generator on a building site, the sounds in the playground during break and dinner time.

Containers special boxes 3, 6, 9 or 12 metres long, and 2.4 metres high and wide. They are used to transport goods on lorries, railways and ships. Goods can be loaded into a container at the factory, and the container then sealed, ready to be delivered.

Decibels the units in which sound is measured — dB for short. 0 dB is absolute silence. 200 dB can cause death.

Defoliate remove the leaves from plants and trees. This sometimes happens "accidentally", as with some air pollution. However, sometimes chemicals are sprayed on to plants in order to defoliate them. It is then easier to clear a large area of jungle or wasteland for farming.

Desalination removing the salt from sea or salt water to make it fit to use for farming or for drinking water.

Drought lack of rain, continuous dry weather.

Ecosystem the plants, animals and the physical environment in a particular area.

Effluent (usually) liquid waste. For example, sewage, waste from a manufacturing process.

Endangered species animals, plants, insects or sea creatures which could become extinct because there are so few of them now.

Environment the surroundings of a plant, animal, insect or sea creature. For example, the environment of a plant depends on the soil, air, climate and weather around it.

Eutrophication the natural aging of a lake. Often this process is speeded up by fertilizers which are washed into the water from the land. Algae grows much more quickly than normal, and the surface of the lake looks like green paint. Because the oxygen is used up by the algae, other living things in the lake die.

Extinct describes a plant, animal, insect or sea creature that has died out completely.

Eyesore something that is ugly and offends the eyes.

Factory farming producing animals for food, rather like a factory. The animals' diet is carefully balanced so that the animals are the size, weight and type that people want to buy. Usually chickens, pigs and veal calves are kept in this way.

Factory ship A special ship which deals with fish and other sea creatures, such as whales, once they have been caught. This allows the fishing ships to catch more. Sometimes a factory ship is called the "mother ship".

Fibrosis lung scarring due to breathing in dust.

Fluorosis a disease which affects cattle. It is caused by cattle eating grass contaminated by fluoride. Fluorosis makes teeth fall out, and bones grow at the joints, so making the cattle lame.

Fly-tipping dumping waste materials illegally. For example, sometimes drums of waste are dumped on waste ground; sometimes lorry drivers leave the taps at the back of their lorry slightly open so that the liquid waste trickles out slowly on the road as the lorry is going along.

Fog this occurs when tiny droplets of water are in the air, making it difficult to see.

Food chain a way in which energy is transferred. Each one in a series of organisms is the food for the next. For example, grass uses the sun's energy to grow, sheep eat the grass, and we eat sheep.

Fossil fuel a source of energy from plants or animals preserved in the earth. Coal, oil and natural gas are all fossil fuels.

Freightliner a service from British Rail which means that a container can be loaded onto the railway line at the factory. The containers are then moved by the railway to their destination. The freightliner service runs to a regular timetable, usually at night.

Frequency of sound the number of times per second that the air particles vibrate back and forwards when a sound is made. Frequency is measured in cycles per second or hertz (Hz).

Green belt area of land around larger towns and cities which is not built on. It is looked on as a "breathing space" for the town.

Green Revolution increasing the yield on farms by use of fertilizers and special "high yield" strains of grain.

Greenhouse effect the way in which heat from the sun may be trapped below a layer of carbon dioxide. This is the same process as in a greenhouse — there the sun is trapped by glass.

Hydro-electric power electricity produced by using a fall of water to drive turbines.

Hypermarket a very large shop, sited out of the town and with its own car park, which sells almost everything — groceries, furniture, clothes, garden materials, and sometimes even cars.

Intensity of sound the amount of energy that vibrating air particles carry to the eardrum.

Intermittent noise unwanted sound that comes and goes. For example, the sound of a pile driver on a building site, a hammer banging in a nail, a chain saw cutting through wood.

Juggernauts the nickname for large articulated lorries.

Minimata Disease a disease caused by mercury poisoning. It produces numbness in the fingers and lips and problems in talking and hearing. People also have difficulties in controlling their arms and legs and may have fits. Children and old people are particularly affected. It is called Minimata Disease after the town of Minimata in Japan where this occurred.

Natural resources the living things, materials and energy on the earth which support our life.

Noise unwanted sound. People have different ideas of what is a noise.

Non-biodegradable describes something which does not break down or rot naturally. For example, most plastic, polystyrene, polythene.

Non-renewable resources resources that cannot be replaced. When they are used, that is the end of them. For example, coal, oil, copper, tin are all non-renewable resources which are used in large quantities and cannot be replaced.

Nuclear energy/power electricity made by using the heat caused by the collision of particles from an atom. Large atoms are not very stable; electrons fly off and collide with other electrons. This process produces heat.

Oil slick a large area of oil floating on the surface of water. It can be many miles in area.

Outfall (pipe) a pipe, usually large, taking waste material into the sea or a river.

Over-fishing taking too many fish out of an area. The remaining fish cannot produce enough young, it will take some years for the area to recover before it can be fished again.

Ozone shield a layer of the gas ozone which surrounds the earth. It acts as a barrier to radiation.

Photochemical smog a special smog which occurs in warm weather. The tiny droplets in the smog irritate the eyes and throat. It is caused by nitrogen dioxide.

Photosynthesis the process in which plants use the energy from the sun to build up complex materials from carbon dioxide and water. In so doing plants use the carbon dioxide which we breathe out and give out oxygen.

Plankton tiny forms of organic life drifting or floating in the sea, rivers and lakes.

Pneumoconiosis a disease caused by breathing in coal dust, where the lungs are scarred.

Pollute, Pollution, Pollutant something which changes the environment for the worse. It may slow down the growth rate of plants and animals; it may be poisonous; it may interfere with a food chain; or it may interfere with people's amenities, health or comfort.

Porous describes something, usually a rock, which has many spaces between the particles so that liquid can pass through.

Radiation rays of light, heat, electromagnetism and so on, coming from a central point. Not all radiation is dangerous.

Radioactive giving off radiation.

Re-cycling reusing something, but not necessarily in its original form. For example, the steel on a car can be used again, but in re-cycling may be used as the steel on a can.

Reservoir a large store of water.

Respiration breathing. In plants, respiration is when carbon dioxide is absorbed and oxygen given off.

Run-off pollutants chemicals which are washed off the land into rivers and the sea. Often these are chemicals which

have been used to produce more food — pesticides and fertilizers.

Sewage farm large area of land over which sewage was allowed to flow. It was hoped that the liquid would gradually become cleaner as it flowed over the ground.

Sewage treatment works area with special buildings for the treatment of sewage.

Silicosis disease caused by breathing in stone dust, where the lungs are scarred.

Smog a fog is when there are so many tiny droplets of water in the air that it is difficult to see. A smog is a fog which contains man-made pollutants.

Smokeless zone an area where there are special restrictions on what fuel can be used. Usually, only gas, oil, electricity or special coal and coke are allowed. There are also restrictions on what industry can burn and give off into the air.

Solar energy power to make electricity using the heat from the sun.

Sonic boom a loud noise caused by the shock waves from an object slamming into the air with no sound warning — for example, Concorde flying faster than the speed of sound.

Sound waves Sound travels through the air in a wave-like motion. Sound disturbing the air is called a sound wave.

Species a group of plants, insects, animals, etc, which are almost the same. They are different in minor details only. For example, people are a species.

Squatters people who live in houses or flats without the owner's permission.

Supersonic faster than the speed of sound, which is 1200 kilometres per hour (760 miles per hour).

Thermal pollution changing the environment for the worse by heat. For example, a power station uses water to cool the reactor. This water, at a warmer temperature, is released into rivers and the sea, and reduces the amount of oxygen in the water.

Third World countries in Africa, Asia and South America which are underdeveloped. They have a lower standard of living than ours. Often they do not have enough to eat, and the medical and health care is poor. People do not live much more than 40 years.

Toxic poisonous.

Waste something that is not wanted and no longer serves a purpose.

Resources List

You can write for further information on environmental topics to these organizations. Make sure that your letter is set out clearly, that you print your name and address, and that you say what information you want. It always helps if you include a stamped addressed envelope.

British Gas Education Service: Education Liaison Officer, British Gas Education Service, Room 414, 326 High Holborn, London WC1V 7PT. For information on energy, gas production, supply and uses.

British Petroleum Company: Educational Service, British Petroleum Company, Britannic House, Moor Lane, London EC2Y 9BU. For information on ecology, energy, pollution control.

British Trust for Conservation Volunteers: National Corps Secretary, British Trust for Conservation Volunteers, 10-14 Duke Street, Reading, Berks. For information on conservation, and practical environmental improvement projects.

British Waterways Board: Senior Press and Publicity Officer, British Waterways Board, Melbury House, Melbury Terrace, London NW1 6JX. For information on transport, history, present uses of waterways and their future.

Compassion in World Farming: Campaign Office, Compassion in World Farming, 20 Lavant Street, Petersfield, Hants GU32 3EW. For information on factory farming, farm animal welfare.

Conservation Trust: Conservation Trust, 246 London Road, Earley, Reading, Berks RG6 1AJ. For information on conservation, pollution, planning, population, waste disposal.

Council for Education in World Citizenship: Director, CEWC, Cobham House, Blackfriars Lane, London EC4V 6EB. For information on conservation, development, environment pollution, world wildlife.

Countryside Commission: Education Officer, Countryside Commission, John Dower House, Crescent Place, Cheltenham, Gloucester GL50 3RA. For information on agriculture, conservation, forestry, land use, planning, recreation, transport, wildlife.

Department of Energy: Department of Energy, Thames House South, Millbank, London SW1P 4QJ. For information on conservation, energy.

Department of The Environment: Public Enquiries Office, Education Service, Directorate of Ancient Monuments and Historic Buildings, 25 Savile Row, London W1X 2BT. For information on buildings, noise, planning, urban conservation, waste disposal.

Department of Transport: Public Enquiries Office, Department of Transport, 2 Marsham Street, London SW1P 3EB. For information on transport, road planning.

Electricity Council: Understanding Electricity, Electricity Council, 30 Millbank, London SW1P 4RD. For information on electricity, power.

Forestry Commission: Information Department, Forestry Commission, 231 Corstorphine Road, Edinburgh EH12 7AT. For information on conservation, forestry.

Friends of the Earth: Friends of the Earth, 377 City Road, London EC1. For information on environmental issues.

Greenpeace: Greenpeace, 6 Endsleigh Street, London WC1. For information on environmental issues, particularly concerned with wildlife, e.g. whales and seals.

Keep Britain Tidy: Education Officer, Bostel House, 37 West Street, Brighton, East Sussex BN1 2RE. For information on litter.

National Coal Board: Schools Services, National Coal Board, Hobart House, Grosvenor Place, London SW1X 7AE. For information on coal, energy, environment.

National Society for Clean Air: Information Office, National Society for Clean Air, 136 North Street, Brighton, East Sussex BN1 1RG. For information on air pollution, noise, waste, water pollution.

National Trust: Junior Division, National Trust, The Old Grape House, Cliveden, Taplow, Maidenhead, Berks SL6 0HZ. For information on conservation, countryside.

National Water Council: National Water Council, 1 Queen Anne's Gate, London SW1H 9BT. For information on water supply, treatment, pollution control, river management. (Also write to your own water authority: find their address in the local telephone book.)

Nature Conservancy Council: Librarian, Nature Conservancy Council, 19-20 Belgrave Square, London SW1X 8PY. For information on nature conservation.

Noise Abatement Society: Hon Secretary, Noise Abatement Society, PO Box 8, Bromley, Kent BR2 0UH. For information on noise.

Overseas Development Administration: Information Department, Overseas Development Administration, Eland House, Stag Place, London SW1 5DH. For information on natural resources, overseas help.

Oxfam: Education Officer, Oxfam, 274 Banbury Road, Oxford, Oxon OX2 7DZ. For information on development, farming, housing, population, water.

Shell UK Ltd: Shell Education Service (UKPA/32), Shell-Mex House, Strand, London WC2R 0DX. For information on oil, environment, energy.

Town and Country Planning Association: Education Officer, Town and Country Planning Association, Education Unit, 17 Carlton House Terrace, London SW1Y 5AS. For information on planning and the built environment.

United Kingdom Atomic Energy Authority: Information Services Branch, 11 Charles II Street, London SW1Y 4QP. For information on nuclear energy.

War on Want: Supporter Services Unit, War on Want, 467 Caledonian Road, London N7 9BE. For information on food production, population.

Watch Trust for Environmental Education: Education Assistant, Watch Trust for Environmental Education, 22 The Green, Nettleham, Lincoln, Lincs LN2 2NR. For information on planning, pollution, wildlife.

World Wildlife Fund: World Wildlife Fund, 29-31 Greville Street, London EC1N 8AX. For information on conservation, wildlife.

Youth Environmental Action: Youth Environmental Action, 173 Archway Road, London N6 5BL. For information on resources, recycling, environment, transport, wildlife.

Index

Figures in **bold type** refer to page numbers of illustrations and captions.